HOMOEOPATHY

A homoeopathic practitioner objectively reviews the strengths and weaknesses of this system of medicine, the potential of which is unlimited and still largely unassessed.

HOMOEOPATHY

The Potent Force of the Minimum Dose

by

Keith A. Scott
M.B., Ch.B., M.F.Hom.

and

Linda A. McCourt
M.A.(Oxon)

Series Editor
George T. Lewith
M.A., M.R.C.G.P., M.R.C.P.

THORSONS PUBLISHERS LIMITED
Wellingborough, Northamptonshire

First published 1982
Third Impression 1985

British Library Cataloguing in Publication Data

Scott, Keith
  Homoeopathy.
  1. Homoeopathy.
  I. Title   II. McCourt, Linda A.
  615.5'32   RX71

  ISBN 0-7225-0780-1
  ISBN 0-7225-0779-8 Pbk

Printed and bound in Great Britain

Contents

Foreword

Dr Samuel Hahnemann described the main precepts of homoeopathy in the nineteenth century, and in spite of its many opponents it has survived for 200 years as a viable and effective system of medicine. In Britain it has received the blessing of the Royal Family and is currently available under the National Health Service in a number of hospitals as well as through a growing band of qualified private practitioners.

The philosophy of homoeopathy has a certain archaic ring about it which makes it difficult for twentieth century man to accept. However, in this book, Dr Scott guides the reader through the confusion and contradictions in this field in a clear and digestible manner.

Biological systems respond in a very marked way to small changes in their environment. Homoeopathy has capitalized on this simple principle by using such small changes to activate and harness the body's own healing potential. Homoeopathy's strength is its evident effectiveness. Its weakness is a lack of scientific evidence to support its mechanism of action, and a dearth of clear statistical data evaluating its efficacy. In spite of these problems this book provides an excellent objective introduction to the subject and allows the reader to make a sound assessment of homoeopathy as an alternative therapy.

GEORGE LEWITH M.A., M.R.C.G.P., M.R.C.P.
Southampton, 1982

Introduction

This is a book about homoeopathy which is free from dogma and prejudice. Homoeopathy, in effect, simply means treating diseases with remedies which are capable of producing symptoms similar to the disease in question when taken by healthy people.

Around this rather stark principle, an edifice of rules and procedures has grown and it is this which we know as the method of homoeopathy today. The method has been built up by remarkable men, all motivated by the highest aim: that of restoring health to sick individuals. However, man is fallible, and excessive zeal can often lead to an uncritical adoption of unfounded assumptions.

This book objectively reviews the strengths and weaknesses of homoeopathy, and its purpose is to stimulate interest in a method of treating disease, the potential of which is unlimited and still largely unassessed.

1. What is Homoeopathy?

The word 'homoeopathy' is derived from the two Greek words, *homois* meaning similar and *pathos* meaning suffering, and their combination represents a very concise description of the homoeopathic method of remedy selection. A remedy selected homoeopathically is chosen because of its ability to produce a range of symptoms in a healthy person similar to that observed in the patient. In other words, the appropriate remedy, in effect, should be able to produce in a healthy person a similar type of suffering to that experienced by the patient.

For example the symptoms of *Belladonna* (Deadly Nightshade) poisoning are well-known, and some of the main effects are wild mania, flushed face, dilated pupils, high fever and a dry mouth without any thirst. Therefore if a patient with an acute illness of some sort presents with the above symptoms, *Belladonna* would be chosen as the appropriate remedy. A flushed face and high fever feature prominently in the symptoms of scarlet fever. In fact there are several recorded examples of the successful treatment of scarlet fever with small doses of *Belladonna*.

Although the approach to disease characteristic of the homoeopathic method has been recognized throughout history, it was a German physician, Samuel Hahnemann (1755-1843), who first experimented with the homoeopathic principle in a sound and methodical way. He also set about systematically 'proving' all the known drugs on healthy people (i.e. recording the complete range of symptoms, mental as well as physical, reported by the healthy person when taking the drug.) He is therefore responsible for the establishment of homoeopathy as a viable alternative to 'allopathy' (derived in part from the Greek word *allos*, meaning other.) Allopathy is an umbrella term used to describe the treatment of disease with remedies that produce effects different from those produced by the disease. It is therefore, as a method, in complete contrast to homoeopathy.

The symptoms exhibited by the patient are of overriding importance in homoeopathy as they indicate the appropriate remedy. It is therefore the task of the homoeopath to record *all* the patient's symptoms, mental and physical. The total symptom picture is then, theoretically, compared with the symptom pictures of the two thousand or so remedies which have been proved so that the one which matches most closely, referred to as the *similimum*, can be found.

The case of arthritis will serve as an illustration of the need to know a whole range of individual symptoms not usually of any interest to the allopathic prescriber. For instance, two women who complain of similar joint stiffness and pain are given totally different remedies because one is frequently sad and listless; her pain is better for continuous gentle movement, warmth, dryness and pressure but worse for cold air, damp, sleep and rest. Her symptoms are similar to the characteristic symptoms of *Rhus toxicodendron* (Poison Ivy). The other woman, however, complains of thirst and has very dry mucous membranes, her pain is worse for movement and pressure but better for rest, cold and open air. Her symptoms are similar to those characteristic of *Bryonia* (Wild Hops).

It is usual to administer remedies selected according to the homoeopathic principle in minute quantities. This practice was instituted by Hahnemann in an attempt to reduce the side-effects associated with taking a 'normal' amount of the remedy. His process of serial (or sequential) dilution of the remedies, which he termed 'potentization', will be discussed later, but it is useful to note that the minute dose is an extension rather than a fundamental part of the homoeopathic principle.

The homoeopathic maxim is often referred to by the Latin phrase *similia similibus curentur*. This translates as "let likes be treated by likes" and illustrates the fact that homoeopathy is essentially a practical clinical method of determining the most appropriate remedy for the patient. It has more in common with a guiding rule than an absolute scientific law, for it is very unusual to discover a true *similimum* (i.e. an identical likeness between a drug picture and a natural disease.) This means that the homoeopath inevitably has to make a value judgment and choose what he considers to be the most significant of the patient's symptoms which require matching. This characteristic of the method makes it difficult to assess the potential of the homoeopathic principle, especially by today's high standards of scientific trials. Thus the evidence in support of homoeopathy is largely anecdotal and, apart from a few 'acceptable' clinical studies, it depends almost totally on the testimony of thousands of practitioners of the art and the even greater number of the laiety who have adopted it as their preferred method of treatment. This should not act as a deterrent to further evaluation of the method but as a good reason to investigate its potential alongside other methods of orthodox treatment so that it may be assigned its rightful place in current medical practices.

2. The History and Formulation of the Homoeopathic Method

The concept of treating like with likes, that is, using remedies which are capable of producing in a healthy person symptoms similar to those seen in the patient in question predates Samuel Hahnemann considerably. Hahnemann never claimed to be the originator of the principle and went to great lengths to point out all the other people who, before him, had suggested it as a means of treatment. However, Hahnemann was certainly the first person to base a system of therapeutics exclusively upon the above principle and he is therefore generally acknowledged to be the founder of homoeopathy. Significant among his predecessors were Hippocrates, and George Ernst Stahl, a Danish physician who lived a century before Hahnemann. Paracelsus has also been mentioned in connection with the homoeopathic principle but Hahnemann felt his own teachings, which were the result of pure observation and experiment, had little to do with the 'unscientific doctrines' and metaphysical speculation of which Paracelsus was so fond.

In Ancient Greece, Hippocrates wrote of symptoms as the expression of Nature's healing powers. For instance, the diarrhoea of dysentery he regarded as Nature's effort to eliminate the poisons responsible for the illness. He therefore urged that treatment should enhance Nature's efforts rather than hinder them, and a purgative rather than a constipating remedy should be given. This concept of disease, that symptoms were the expression of the healing force (the *Vis Medicatrix*

Naturae), was consistent with the generally held belief at that time that Nature was a Goddess and any symptoms of disease therefore belonged to the realm of her Divine wisdom.

George Ernst Stahl wrote in the seventeenth century: 'The rule generally acted upon in medicine . . . to treat by means of opposite acting remedies *(Contraria Contrariis)* is the reverse of what it ought to be: I am, on the contrary, convinced that disease will yield to, and be cured by, remedies that produce similar affections!' This is a direct pronunciation of the homoeopathic principle.

It is difficult to assess whether Paracelsus actually pronounced the homoeopathic principle as such for his teachings are wrapped in obscurity. He worked from the basic assumption that there were correspondences between the microcosm and the macrocosm and that man (the microcosm) contained within him all the forms of external nature (the macrocosm). Every diseased organ, therefore, had its corresponding remedy in nature; these remedies he called the external organs. Thus a certain herb would be categorized as a 'heart' because it acted primarily on the heart. Rejecting the *Contraria Contrariis* principle he declared that 'sames must be cured by sames'. This sounds like a pronunciation of the homoeopathic principle, yet he wrote that the key to understanding the inner properties of a remedy lay in the outward characteristics of that remedy and these were to be discovered using intuitive rather than rational thinking. In other words it is unlikely that the remedies were chosen because they could produce, in a healthy person, similar symptoms to those being treated. This is by no means the final word for there are many people who are of the view that a substantial part of his medical practice was based on the homoeopathic principle.

Samuel Hahnemann

Samuel Hahnemann was born in Meissen, Germany, in 1755. He should have followed his father in the trade of porcelain-painting, but his aptitude for scholarly work was so impressive that his school teachers, in order that he should continue his schooling, agreed to remit his fees. In 1775, at the age of twenty, with little money, but with the ability to speak eight languages, he set off for the University of Leipzig to study medicine. Two

Photo: courtesy A. Nelson & Co. Ltd.

Bronze bust of Samuel Hahnemann by Woltreck (1839).

years later he moved to Vienna in search of practical facilities for his study which were not available at Leipzig, and there he taught languages and translated articles in order to stave off the ever-present threat of penury. He obtained his degree of Doctor of Medicine in 1779. He married soon after and from that time onwards his life was one of incessant movement. He and his wife and their ever-increasing family moved twenty times in twenty years, an incredible feat considering the conditions prevalent at the end of the eighteenth century. He continued translating articles, as his financial position was seldom secure, especially as compassion tended to overrule business sense when charging his patients. Despite these conditions he never faltered in his ceaseless quest for knowledge in a wide range of subjects, particularly medicine. He was able to talk and write authoritatively in several languages, on subjects ranging from philology to ecclesiastical history.

Although he moved frequently, he acquired a reputation for being a conscientious and careful physician who was devoted to the task of helping his patients in the most efficacious and harmless way possible. After he 'stumbled' on the homoeopathic principle his career became even more chequered, with praises, accolades and veneration rivalling abuse, ridicule and scorn. He survived to his eighty-eighth year when he died in Paris, content that his life had not been in vain. His homoeopathic practice was, at the time of his death, the most famous in Europe. Dukes, Princes, and Politicians, as well as the poor, all flocked daily to his Rue de Milan surgery for treatment.

Hahnemann's Initial Theories

Although the homoeopathic principle was basically conceived as the result of an experiment on himself, with the then well known drug Cinchona bark, it is interesting to note his ideas on disease for they enabled him to grasp immediately the full potential and scope inherent in the homoeopathic principle.

Hahnemann's attitude towards the treatment of disease diverged from the mainstream very early in his career. In fact, he went so far as to say that there were few diseases in the treatment of which his contemporary physicians did no harm. He was appalled at the haphazard way in which physicians experimented on their patients with complex prescriptions of up to ten drugs at a time. For instance, of the two drugs very commonly employed, Mercury and Cinchona bark, he said: 'If so great an obscurity reigns with regard to these single drugs, how useless must be the phenomena which appear after the indiscriminate administration of several such drugs together.' Hahnemann always tried to administer drugs singly, and would never repeat them until he felt sure that their action, which he observed closely, had been exhausted. In this way he hoped to establish a set of reliable indications for the use of different drugs.

While his fellow physicians devoted their energies to writing prescriptions, he took detailed case histories. He made enquiries into the condition of his patients' living quarters and the nature of their work, and he urged cleanliness at a time when the concept of hygiene was unknown. He considered 'a strengthening diet, wholesome air and exercise, together with amusement to the mind' to be essential to health. His sensitivity and concern are best illustrated by his views on the treatment of insanity. During Hahnemann's time, refractory, maniacal patients were treated like wild animals and a well fitted 'madhouse' was not unlike a torture-chamber. Hahnemann said of this: 'I never allow an insane person to be punished either by blows or any other kind of corporal chastisement because there is no punishment where there is no responsibility, and because these sufferers deserve only pity and are always rendered worse by such rough treatment and never improved.'

Hahnemann's radical attitude towards venesection (bleeding the patient) did not endear him to most of the profession as it was their most cherished method of treatment and considered to be essential for 'resolving obstructions, expelling acridities and evil humours and removing the morbidly overproduced, accumulated inflammatory blood from organs.' Although he bled his patients in the early part of his career he soon came to regard it with as much contempt as he regarded those who employed it. Unfortunately when Hahnemann introduced his homoeopathic method his critics whipped up resistance to it by making homoeopathy appear to be synonomous with a refusal to bleed; a concept no physician at that time could entertain.

Discovery of the Homoeopathic Principle

The foregoing account, even to a prejudiced reader, clearly singles out Hahnemann as an original, sensitive and logical scientist and one of those rare men who was able to throw off limiting orthodox beliefs in order to look for better explanations. Hahnemann always stressed the need to know accurately all the effects of the different drugs in use, and this need led him ultimately to experiment on himself. He first experimented with Cinchona bark, a remedy commonly used in cases of so-called intermittent fever (intermittent fever was, in fact, malaria.) He took substantial doses of the bark for a couple of days and described the effects as follows:

> My feet, finger tips etc. first grew cold, I became exhausted and sleepy, then my heart began to palpitate, my pulse became hard and rapid, I had intolerable anxiety, trembling prostration in all my limbs, then throbbing in the head, flushing of the cheeks, thirst and, in short, all the ordinary symptoms of intermittent fever.

Cinchona officinalis

Gemahlt von Schoppe 1831.   Stahlstich v. Leop. Beyer in Wien.

Samuel   *Hahnemann*

geboren den   *10. Aprill 1755.*

With compliments

Samuel Hahnemann 1755-1843. From a steel engraving by Leopold Beyer, b. Vienna 1784 – d. after 1870; after the oil painting of 1831 by Julius Schoppe the elder, b. Berlin 1795 – d. 1868. Schoppe was professor of the Berlin Academy 1836 and decorated the residence of Prince Charles at Glienicke near Potsdam

Hahnemann was able to attest to the resemblance as he had, in fact, suffered from malaria when he was younger. He concluded from this experiment that the bark overpowered and eradicated the intermittent fever chiefly by exciting a fever of short duration of its own. In an article on venereal disease he said that mercury (commonly used in the treatment of syphilis) had a counter-irritant action on the body. He referred to its most developed form as mercurial fever and remarked that mercurial fever was similar to the symptoms of syphilis, although he had not yet pronounced the homoeopathic principle.

He first alluded to the homoeopathic principle in an article in 1796 in the leading medical journal in Germany. In this article he wrote that in choosing a remedy, one must imitate nature and employ in the disease one wishes to cure, 'that medicine which is able to produce another very similar artificial disease.' From this time onwards he became increasingly occupied with the construction of a system of therapeutics based on this principle. This dedication and enthusiasm are understandable for suddenly there was no longer any need to conduct haphazard experiments on patients. If all the known drugs and many more could be 'proved' on healthy people then the resulting drug pictures would supply specific and accurate indications for their use. One would simply have to match a patient's symptom picture with an appropriate drug picture.

The Organon

He soon gathered a band of devoted followers and set about 'proving' certain well-known drugs on them and on his family. He also examined toxicological data as these he considered to be acceptable, if accidental, provings. The result of all this earnest activity was his *Materia Medica Pura* which is a compilation of all the differing drug pictures he had obtained from the provings. In 1810 his *Organon of Rational Medicine* (later changed to *The Organon of the Healing Art*) appeared; it was the first of five editions. Each edition shows considerable changes and is a testament to the evolution of his ideas on the subject and the practice of homoeopathy. It is certainly worthwhile, if not essential, to describe the contents of the *Organon* for it is, in essence, Hahnemann's exposition and vindication of his therapeutic method. Although homoeopathy has evolved to a certain extent, and different schools of thought have developed, the homoeopathy practised today is still largely that advocated by Hahnemann, and his *Organon* is still, therefore, the most authoritative work on the subject.

Hahnemann introduced new concepts in the different editions but all editions have a similar outline and structure. The first part of the *Organon* is concerned with a discussion and illustration of his ideas concerning the basic desiderata on which the practice of medicine depends; the knowledge of the disease, the knowledge of medicinal powers and the knowledge of how to choose and administer the remedy. The second part is concerned with the procedures necessary to gain the appropriate knowledge. Rules are given on the examination of the patient, the proving of drugs, the determination of similarity, the choice and repetition of the dose, the preparation of the remedies and the diet and regimen to be observed.

As far as a knowledge of the disease was concerned Hahnemann concluded that the sum total of the patient's symptoms, emotional and physical, was the only curative indication available to the physician. However, where one could discover an 'exciting and maintaining cause' this was to be excluded if possible. This is why he attached such importance to diet, hygiene and the psychological situation, and in so doing acknowledged the role of 'preventive' medicine; something not considered in his day.

The position he took with regard to the knowledge of drug action was far less controversial. By insisting on 'proving' drugs on healthy human bodies he is perhaps the father of experimental pharmacology. The advantage of experimenting with humans is that subjective as well as objective clinical symptoms can be ascertained. The disadvantage is that incidental symptoms having nothing to do with the actual drug action may also be reported. Hahnemann recognized this disadvantage and in the rules which he set up for proving drugs, he attempted to minimize this error.

As far as the method of selecting a remedy was concerned he argued that the homoeopathic way was the only one to treat diseases, especially those of a chronic nature. His criticisms of what he considered to be the two alternative methods available are as valid today as they were then. He had two major objections to the first method, 'allopathy' (i.e. the treatment of disease by remedies that produce effects different from those produced by the disease.) The first objection concerned the uncertainty of the method in that one could not be sure whether it would have the desired effect, and one was therefore only guessing at the problem rather than solving it. The second objection was that it was actually harmful because it disordered healthy tissue and flooded the system with large amounts of sometimes very poisonous substances.

The second method which he called the 'antipathic method' involved an attempt to neutralize various symptoms by giving remedies which produced directly opposing effects; for example, giving purgatives in constipation, alkalis in conditions of excess acidity etc. He acknowledged the effectiveness of antipathic drugs in many acute conditions but stressed their inadequacy in the treatment of chronic and recurrent diseases. In his words, "the vain empiric imagines it to be the beaten highway and plumes himself on the wretched power of giving but a few hours' ease, unconcerned if, during this specious calm, the disease plants its roots still deeper." It is indeed hard to find a more eloquent and accurate objection to the antipathic method. According to Hahnemann it was also limited in that there were relatively few directly opposing states which existed between natural disease and drug action, and furthermore it was inadequate in that it was usually limited to the treatment of single symptoms.

Homoeopathy, according to Hahnemann, was the superior method on many counts. It acted directly on the affected parts, that is the remedies were 'target specific'. It was gentle in its manner because of the very small doses he came to favour and employ. It was also of 'inexhaustable fertility' in that any disease which presented itself, known or unknown, could be treated simply by finding a drug picture which matched as accurately as possible the specific disease picture. He became so enthusiastic over this point that he even wanted to see the naming and classification of diseases abolished. His uncompromising, almost missionary zeal alienated him even further from his colleagues who were attempting during that time, through pathological studies in their 'dead-houses', to distinguish and classify diseases. Critics of homoeopathy have always belaboured its 'obsessive' attention to symptoms and its almost total disregard of actual diagnosis. However, to criticize this point unduly is to misunderstand Hahnemann's very noble objective which was to be able to remedy destructive processes occuring in the body before they actually manifested as gross pathological changes. He thus regarded the totality of a patient's symptoms as the only available indication of such processes.

The practical advice contained in the *Organon* will be discussed in the relevant chapters. However, it is important at this stage to briefly digress and trace Hahnemann's ideas on what constituted a suitable dose, as his conclusions were almost more revolutionary, and therefore harder to accept, than the homoeopathic principle itself.

The Concept of Potentization

At the beginning of his career he administered drugs in the accepted doses, although even then he differed from his colleagues in that, in the case of the powerful drugs, he gave small doses initially and gradually increased them until his patients showed slight signs of toxicity, he would then discontinue them until these signs disappeared. He gradually started to favour smaller doses and in his *Treatise on a New Principle* in 1796 he advised the administration of a dose just strong enough to produce a scarcely perceptible indication of the expected artificial disease.

The dilution of the remedies was a natural extension of his desire to reduce the side-effects experienced when giving larger doses. He found that sometimes even very small doses acted more strongly than was desirable and he therefore proceeded still further in the diminution of the dose. As it became practically impossible to keep dividing the crude drug substance, he developed a particular method of achieving dilutions hitherto unheard of in the history of pharmacy. He called this particular process 'potentization', as his observation and experience led him to the conclusion that diluting the remedies in this way, far from diminishing their overall effect as he had expected, actually enhanced their 'curative powers'. He came to believe that the more one diluted the remedy the more potent it became. Obviously this conclusion stunned the disbelieving world, and today it still represents the most indigestible part of the homoeopathic method especially when one considers that after a certain amount of dilution the remedy technically is no longer detectable in a material form (i.e. in molecules). Whether our current state of scientific knowledge throws any light on this fundamental aspect of the homoeopathic method will be examined in a later chapter.

Theories on the Homoeopathic Principle

Hahnemann, predictably, was not content with the homoeopathic principle alone and he put forward several theories to account for the success he achieved using the principle. However, it is important to realize that he never attached much significance to them and he certainly never castigated any converts to homoeopathy if they did not subscribe to any of these theories. Hahnemann was reputed to have said, 'I can only vouch for the what and not the how.'

One of his theories was that the naturally occurring disease was removed by the action of a similar, artificially induced, drug disease, the latter of which was short-lived. In Hahnemann's words, 'when the two irritations greatly resemble each other, then the one weaker irritation, together with its effects will be completely extinguished and annihilated by the analogous power of the other (the stronger).' It is interesting to note in this connection, as Hahnemann himself noted, that it is a fairly common clinical observation for an established disease to vanish during an intercurrent illness; in other words, that one disease does appear sometimes, temporarily at least, to displace another.

Another theory revolved around his ideas on the mode of action of drugs. Hahnemann wrote, 'most medicines have more than one action, the first a direct action, which gradually changes into the second (which I shall call the indirect secondary action). The latter is generally a state exactly the opposite of the former. If, in a case of chronic disease, the indirect secondary action is sometimes exactly the state of the body sought to be brought about.' In this reasoning lies a small intellectual coup for it explains simultaneously why antipathic remedies are not desirable and why homoeopathic remedies *are* desirable. Theoretically, then, antipathic remedies, although initially antagonistic in their action, are followed by an opposing secondary action which is similar to the disease itself and the condition is eventually made worse. On the other hand, the primary action of homoeopathic remedies is similar to the disease while its secondary action is antagonistic to the disease and a state of health is thereafter regained. A secondary, totally different action of a substance is not unknown, one only needs to think of how the initial elevating effects of alcohol can eventually become those euphemistically referred to as a 'hang-over'.

Vital Force

His final theory involved the concept of a vital force which, in the latter part of his life, he believed to be the source of all phenomena of life. He postulated that it became deranged during illness and he suggested that homoeopathically selected remedies stimulated this flagging vital force so that, in the words of Hahnemann, 'it can again take the reins and conduct the system on the way to health.'

Clearly these theories are inadequate and, although Hahnemann developed a propensity for speculating in the murkier realms of hypothesis in his later years (something he abhored in his earlier years) he was definitely a man who preferred rigorous observation and experiment and would undoubtably have wanted the homoeopathic principle to be judged in this way rather than by the theories put forward in explanation of it.

Hahnemann is not the only one to attempt to theorize on the subject; subsequent generations of homoeopaths have also produced theories. This need to explain the homoeopathic principle is understandable and obvious for it is easy for most people to grasp the concepts underlying allopathic and antipathic methods, but to conceive of a disease being effectively treated with a remedy which is capable of producing a similar disease pattern is certainly difficult for most people.

Chronic Disease and Miasms

Finally it is necessary to briefly describe Hahnemann's later views on chronic disease, for experience showed him that well selected homoeopathic remedies often failed to have any effect in chronic diseases. It was known in Hahnemann's day that a

few chronic conditions were traceable to venereal infection—
syphilitic or sycotic (gonorrheal). He therefore postulated that
the large remaining proportion of chronic diseases must also
have some direct association with a particular disease. After
scouring through all the available medical literature he found
numerous observations of chronic conditions following the
suppression of various skin eruptions among which scabies, or
'itch', was the most prevalent. He called this specific range of
disorders 'psora' and announced that the majority of chronic
diseases had their origins in psoric affections, the remaining ones
having their origins in syphilis or sycosis (gonorrhea).

He called these affections 'miasms,' a word which is derived
from the Greek word *miainein* meaning 'to pollute'. This is why
one will find frequent reference in homoeopathic literature to
the three different 'miasms' and the remedies which Hahnemann
decided, in an empirical fashion, effectively treated the miasms
and their associated chronic conditions. Many people,
homoeopaths included, rejected this doctrine (and still do) and
his critics have incessantly seized upon it in order to ridicule
homoeopathy, although his 'Miasmic Theory' has nothing to do
with the fundamental tenets of homoeopathy.

There has been a revival in the concept of miasms although it
has been broadened to include the possibility that almost any
illness, although 'successfully' treated at the time, can be
associated with residual effects which predispose the body to
certain chronic conditions. It is interesting to note, in this
respect, that it is common for people to be able to trace back the
beginnings of a non-specific chronic complaint to a specific
illness after which they had 'never really been the same.'

The Spread of the Homoeopathic Method

The foregoing account describes the essence of Hahnemann's
homoeopathic theory, although his practical advice contained
in the *Organon* is still to be discussed in the appropriate
chapters. It only remains, in the conclusion of this chapter, to
trace the course of his method from the time he announced it to
the present day. It would be worthwhile to begin with a
quotation from Hahnemann written in 1815, when only a few
isolated doctors in Saxony were among his adherents:

Our art requires no political lever, no worldly decorations in order to become something. It grows gradually, at first unrecognized, surrounded as it were by all manner of weeds which luxuriate around it, from an insignificant acorn to a sapling, soon its summit will overtop the rank weeds. Patience! It is striking deep its roots into the earth, it is increasing in strength imperceptibly but all the more surely and will in its own time grow into an oak of God, which no longer shaken by storms, spreads out its branches into all regions that suffering mankind may be healed under its beneficient shade.

Such was Hahnemann's confidence and conviction in his method and he actually lived to see thousands of practitioners, some of great repute, convert to homoeopathy, and millions of people enthusiastically embrace the method.

These gains were not without a great deal of sacrifice on the part of the converts. Hahnemann personally suffered much abuse and he was eventually exiled from Leipzig because of a successful action brought against him by the Apothecaries who resented him making and dispensing his own medicines. Hahnemann was not blameless in the raging public debate of homoeopathy versus other methods which degenerated into a succession of calumnies, and even the respectable medical journals succumbed. An example of the type of comments which were eventually being made against homoeopathy well illustrates the depths to which the debate had sunk. 'Homoeopathy must appear to every rational being to be the excrement of a mind whose brain has suffered decomposition in the living body.' Hahnemann meanwhile, became increasingly dogmatic, abusive and uncompromising and refused to acknowledge a place for any of the current allopathic practices; homoeopathy was the answer to everything!

Unfortunately this unbending stance of Hahnemann's may well have set a precedent for his followers, and bigotry has never been a very successful platform from which to launch new ideas, concepts and methods. Indeed the history of homoeopathy may well be described as a history of bigotry especially where the attitudes and tactics of the orthodox profession were concerned. The words of Dr Dudgeon written in 1885 are worth quoting for they are almost as appropriate now as they were then:

It must strike every unprejudiced observer as a very hopeless way of suppressing a novel system of therapeutics, to abuse and calumnate its author, to persecute its adherents by criminal processes, coroner's inquests, expulsion from medical societies, deprivation of hospital appointments, exclusion from periodical literature and social and professional ostracism. One would think that the right way would be to afford them opportunities in hospitals to test its value side by side with traditional methods, to court discussion in societies and periodicals, to make careful experiments with remedies . . .

Homoeopathy, however, soon spread from Germany to Austria where it made such an impact that objectors managed to obtain an Imperial decree forbidding its practice in 1819. However, it re-asserted itself so strongly that this edict was rescinded in 1837. Soon it had also spread to Italy, France, England and its colonies of India, Canada and Australia, Spain, Portugal, Holland, Belgium, Switzerland, Russia and America. The spread occurred relatively rapidly and most of the above countries had established homoeopathic journals and even hospitals before the turn of the century (1900). However, very little real progress was made because of the prejudice encountered by adherents of the homoeopathic method, and the demand for homoeopathy has tended to wax and wane. The interest has also depended, to a certain extent, on the characteristics of the men who adopted the method; if they were charismatic, well-esteemed and energetic, interest grew; if they were introverted and had little public appeal, interest waned. This unfortunately will continue to happen as long as homoeopathy is forced to remain a 'fringe' method, and until it is properly assessed alongside orthodox methods it will never become integrated into the fabric of orthodox medical practices.

The pattern was notably different in America, at least initially, as minds were much more open and accustomed to change. The number of homoeopathic practitioners grew from one in 1825 to about 9,500 in 1900, in other words, 20-25 per cent of all physicians practised homoeopathy at the turn of the century. Over one hundred hospitals and teaching centres were established in many cities. However, as the sciences of anatomy, bacteriology, physiology and pharmacology developed, exciting new developments and drugs which appeared on the scene proved to be too much of a contrast for the rather gentle, non-invasive approach of homoeopathy, and prejudice set in once more.

James Kent

Mention must be made of an American homoeopath, James Kent (1849-1916), who, in his own right, gave a much needed impetus to homoeopathy. Although Kent practised homoeopathy mainly in accordance with the Hahnemannian tradition he became responsible for the institutionalization of two different practices, (this particular brand of homoeopathy is referred to as 'Kentian Homoeopathy'.) Kent adopted the use of remedies in potencies far greater than those employed or even conceived of, by Hahnemann. His other practice was to give priority to the constitutional symptoms of a patient (the physical and dispositional characteristics) when selecting an appropriate remedy, although he never lost sight of the Hahnemannian objective of matching, as far as possible, the total range of symptoms.

The next few chapters will elaborate on those subjects only briefly referred to in this chapter; potency, the *Materia Medica*, and case-taking. The scientific evidence in support of homoeopathy will be assessed and conditions which are suitable for homoeopathic treatment will be discussed as well as the position of homoeopathy in England today.

3. How Homoeopathic Remedies Are Made

Homoeopathic remedies manufactured today are still made in accordance with the strict rules Hahnemann laid down in his *Materia Medica Pura*. This is important as there is evidence that his particular technique is crucial to the common clinical observation that increasing dilutions produce remedies which, under certain circumstances, are increasingly potent or effective. The evidence in support of this contention will be discussed after the manufacturing processes have been described.

The first stage involves the preparation of liquid 'mother tinctures' symbolized by the Greek letter ϕ. These tinctures, which contain the various remedies in their most concentrated form, are prepared by steeping the appropriate botanical, or less frequently animal, substance in an alcohol solution for periods of up to one month. The mixture is then thoroughly pressed and filtered and the resultant solution is called the 'mother tincture'. Minerals which are totally soluble in alcohol or water are not subjected to the above process; the pure substance is used as the equivalent starting point.

The successive dilutions, or potencies as they are called, are then made from the appropriate mother tincture or pure mineral using either the centesimal scale (Hahnemann's choice) or less commonly the decimal scale. The first potency (1c) on the centesimal scale is made by adding one part of mother tincture or pure mineral to 99 parts of an alcohol solution. The mixture is then succussed (shaken vigorously). Today this is achieved

Photo: courtesy A. Nelson & Co. Ltd.

Natural substances stored in readiness for making mother tinctures.

using a machine which succusses the solution in a container through repeated impact with a solid surface. Hahnemann used to bang the vial containing the solution on a sturdy leatherbound book. To achieve the second potency (2c) one part of this mixture is added to 99 parts of the alcohol solution which is then again succussed. This process can be continued indefinitely in order to achieve the desired potency.

In the decimal series, the first potency (1x) is made by diluting one part of mother tincture or pure mineral with 9 parts of the alcohol solution followed by succussion. The second potency (2x) is made by adding one part of the first potency mixture to 9 parts of the alcohol solution whi:h is once more subjected to the succussion process and so on. Remedies which have been diluted according to the decimal scale are written as follows: 1x, 2x, 3x, etc. Sometimes they are designated with a 'D' e.g. 1D, 2D, 3D. Remedies diluted according to the centesimal scale are either written simply as 1, 2, 3, etc. or as 1c, 2c, 3c, etc.

The following table compares the two series with the actual dilution ratio and it will be obvious that the potency refers to the number of diluting and succussing stages the remedy has been through rather than the particular degree of dilution. This is significant when considered in the light of Hahnemann's belief, for which there is now some evidence, that succussion, in conjunction with dilution, is crucial to the apparent increase in the clinical effect of the remedy with increasing dilution. Thus 24x is of a higher potency than 12c. Although they are technically diluted to the same degree the 24x remedy has been through 12 additional stages of dilution and succussion.

Dilution Ratio	Decimal Series	Centesimal Series
1/10 or 10^{-1}	1x	—
1/100 or 10^{-2}	2x	1c
1/1,000 or 10^{-3}	3x	—
1/10,000 or 10^{-4}	4x	2c
10^{-12}	12x	6c
10^{-24}	24x	12c
10^{-60}	60x	30c
$10^{-2,000}$	not made	M (equivalent to 1,000c)
$10^{-20,000}$	not made	10M (equivalent to 10,000c)
$10^{-200,000}$	not made	CM (equivalent to 100,000c)

If the particular remedy to be potentized is insoluble in both alcohol and water; for example, silica and gold, then, to achieve a 1c potency, one part of the substance is added to 99 parts of sugar of milk (lactose) and finely ground using a pestle and mortar. One part of this mixture is then added to 99 parts of sugar of milk and finely ground in order to obtain a 2c potency

Photo: courtesy A. Nelson & Co. Ltd.

Preparing homoeopathic potencies.

and so on. This process is called 'trituration' and can be repeated indefinitely to obtain the full range of potencies.

Hahnemann, however, saw reason to believe that after the third stage of trituration the substance became, for practical purposes, soluble. He therefore instructed potencies of insoluble substances above 3c to be made as described above using the dilution and succussion processes. Hahnemann at that time only had recourse to observation and experiment to assure himself of the validity of this assumption. He was certainly unaware of the existence of 'colloids' and it now appears that his process of prolonged trituration converts insoluble substances into a colloidal state. In this state they can be suspended in a fluid medium indefinitely and behave from a practical pharmaceutical standpoint as solutions.

When the required potency has been reached, the alcohol solution containing the potentized remedy is added to a specified quantity of sugar of milk which is then made up into little white tablets or left in a powder form. The remedies can also be prepared in granule form, derived from a sucrose as opposed to a lactose base. Ointments and suppositories are also made up, although these usually contain the appropriate remedy in tincture form rather than potency. The most commonly employed potencies in clinical practice are as follows: 1x, 3x, 6x, 12x and 6c, 12c, 30c, 200c, 1M, 10M and CM.

Possible Relevance of the Arndt-Schultz Law

The burning question now arises: what evidence is there to justify the use of small doses and the contention that increasing dilutions are associated, to some extent, with an increasing therapeutic effect? The Arndt-Schultz Law, in reference to general biological activity, states that large stimuli tend to harm or destroy, lesser stimuli tend to inhibit while small stimuli tend to encourage. For example, large amounts of arsenic acid will kill a yeast culture, lesser amounts will impair its fermentative activity while small amounts will, for a time at least, encourage the fermentation process.

This law, to some extent, vindicates Hahnemann's preference for small doses which he believed were not only less harmful but were ultimately more effective than larger doses. Additionally there is evidence that diseased tissue is far more sensitive to various stimuli than it would be if it were healthy. Hahnemann realized this and, with regard to the use of small doses, wrote in 1830:

A medicine homoeopathically chosen . . . affects only the diseased parts of the organism, therefore, just the most irritated extremely sensitive part of it. Therefore its dose must be so small as to affect the diseased part just a little more than the disease itself did. For this the smallest dose suffices—one so small as to be incapable of altering the

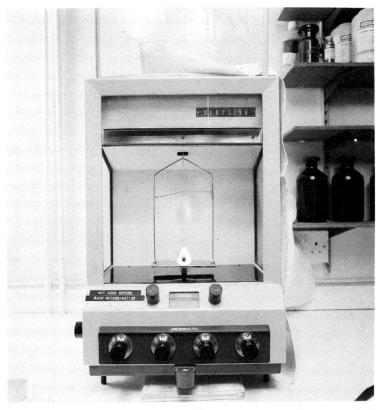

Photo: courtesy A. Nelson & Co. Ltd.

Precision balances used in the manufacture of homoeopathic medicines.

health of a healthy person, or of making him ill, which only larger doses of medicine can do.

This quotation reveals great perception and suggests the possible mechanism whereby remedies prescribed according to the *similimum* principle are effective in the treatment of disease, yet those taken through inappropriate prescription or misadventure generally prove to be harmless. (See chapter on *Materia Medica* for further details.)

Photo: courtesy A. Nelson & Co. Ltd.

Modern quality control equipment for measuring refractive indices.

Scientific Evidence of the Activity of High Potencies

The real difficulty in explaining the concept of the minimum dose arises from the fact that the dilutions greater than 10^{-23} can no longer possibly contain any molecules of the original remedy. This can be deduced from Avogadro's Law which states that the number of molecules in one gramme-molecule is 6.023×10^{-23}. In other words potencies above 12c and 24x (see table) contain no hint of the remedy in a material form. However, the late Dr W. E. Boyd spent many years carefully testing and assessing the effect on biological activity of dilutions of substances, prepared in the homoeopathic manner, which exceeded the Avogadro limit of 10^{23}. In 1954 he delivered what is now a classic paper on the 'Evidence of Activity of High Potencies'. In this paper he described how dilutions of up to 10^{-60} of mercuric acid, when compared with the control situation using distilled water, still had a statistically significant stimulating effect on the activity of the enzyme diastase, which breaks down starch through the process of hydrolysis.

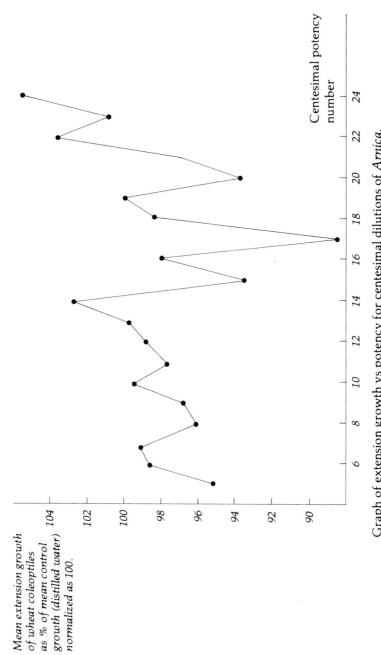

Mean extension growth of wheat coleoptiles as % of mean control growth (distilled water) normalized as 100.

Centesimal potency number

Graph of extension growth vs potency for centesimal dilutions of *Arnica*.

Courtesy The British Homoeopathic Journal

Effect of Potentized Substances on Wheat Seedlings

Furthermore, a recent experiment on the effect of high and low potencies on wheat seedling growth, not only confirms Boyd's conclusions, but also arrives at several other equally significant conclusions. Drs Jones and Jenkins, working at the Royal London Homoeopathic Hospital, have demonstrated that homoeopathic remedies, depending on their particular potency, can have a stimulating or inhibiting effect on the growth of wheat seedlings when compared with the control situation in which distilled water only is used. More significantly they have been able to reproduce their results, something which previous experiments on plant growth have failed to do. The graph on page 38 illustrates the effect of *Arnica*, in different potencies, on the growth of wheat seedlings.

The graph clearly demonstrates that some potencies definitely inhibit growth while others stimulate growth, all to varying degrees. A number of other remedies, in varying potencies, produce different characteristic growth curves. Although it would be totally unjustified to extrapolate these results to the clinical situation, they do seem to corroborate the common clinical experience that well-matched remedies often fail to have any effect in one particular potency but will have the desired effect in another potency. Yet, as the plant experiment experience shows, the higher potencies are not always associated with greater effect.

Clearly Hahnemann was justified in assuming that his process of dilution, far from diminishing the power of the remedy, actually gave the remedy new attributes. For instance, some of the most cherished and most effective homoeopathic remedies are *Natrum muriaticum* (common salt), *Silica* (flint), *Carbo vegetabilis* (burnt vegetable matter) and *Carbo animalis* (burnt animal matter). All of these substances have a negligible effect in their crude state yet clinical experience testifies to their often remarkable powers when prescribed homoeopathically in the potentized form. However, it appears that the apparent increase in the clinical effect of potentized remedies does not seem to follow the simple linear progression suggested by the potency series.

Hahnemann decided that the number of succussive stages and the length of the triturative process determined the ultimate effectiveness and power of the remedy. Two further findings in the above experiment substantiate his belief, at least as far as the succussion process is concerned. Firstly, when the effects on the growth rate of the centessimal range of potencies were compared with those of the decimal range, the trends were found to be similar. This means, for example, that 12x and 12c elicited similar responses from the wheat seedlings. As mentioned previously the potency refers to the number of successive stages rather than the actual degree of dilution; 12c is a more diluted form of the remedy than 12x. This result implies that the number of successive stages is of overriding importance. In other words, the process of shaking during dilution is crucial in determining the ultimate effect of the potentized remedy.

Secondly, aqueous potencies of a certain remedy were kept at room temperature for seven days and were then employed in a similar experiment. The resultant growth figures did not differ in any way from those obtained using distilled water only. However, when these solutions were re-succussed, values comparable with the initial results were obtained. This suggests that the loss of 'activity' of the remedy can be restored by simply shaking the solution. It must be mentioned here that this loss of 'activity' does not seem to occur in potentized remedies which have been made up into their respective tablet, powder or granule form.

Inability to Explain the Phenomenon of Potentization
No attempt shall be made to describe any of the complicated theories put forward in explanation of the potentization phenomenon. However, it may be useful to view all these findings, as well as many others, in terms of energy rather than mass, a conclusion which science is generally reaching. Hahnemann likened the process to the generation of heat through friction. It may well be that the forced mechanical incorporation of remedy molecules, which have a different size, configuration and range of properties, into the diluent molecule structure (through succussion and trituration) sets up energy stresses which may be perpetuated in the diluent medium long after the remedy ceases to exist in a material form. All of the theories advanced are still speculative and a lot more work needs

to be done. Nevertheless the important consideration is that high potencies have a demonstrable effect on life-activity (many other independent experiments testify to this fact) and this means that the concept of the homoeopathic 'minute' dose should be more thoroughly investigated.

4. The Materia Medica

The homoeopathic *Materia Medica* is a compilation of the various remedies with their characteristic symptoms and indications for use. The remedies are listed alphabetically and are generally known by their Latin names, a practice which is necessary to avoid confusion. Most of the more recent *Materia Medicas* have adopted the format used by Hahnemann in his *Materia Medica Pura* and later in his *Chronic Diseases.* In these he distributed the symptoms obtained from the 'provings' and other sources into different schemes, mainly anatomical, proceeding from the head to the extremities. Additional schemes contained information about the general and mental characteristics of the remedy.

Boericke's *Materia Medica* is the most widely used today and, following Hahnemann, he categorized the symptoms under the headings: Mind, Head, Eyes, Ears, Nose, Face, Mouth, Throat, Stomach, Abdomen, Stool, Urine, Male, Female, Respiratory, Heart, Back, Extremities, Sleep, Fever, Skin and finally Modalities (those factors which either relieve or aggravate the symptoms). Each remedy description begins with a discussion on the general effects and characteristics, and often includes suggestions as to the type of person that particular remedy would suit. We describe below some of the main symptoms typical of *Sepia*, the inky juice from the cuttle fish, so that the astounding variety and the type of information required by the homoeopathic practitioner may be more fully appreciated.

Typical Example of a Remedy Description

SEPIA

Generalities
Sepia is particularly suited to female brunettes who are tall, thin and of sallow complexion. There is general weakness and debility. An important remedy at the menopause and in uterine conditions. Great flushes of heat which begin below and move upwards, followed by intense sweating.

MIND: Indifferent to those loved most; apathetic; averse to consolation but dreads solitude; very sensitive and easily offended; weepy; lack of sexual interest.

HEAD: Falling out of hair (Alopecia); severe headaches—relieved by sleep.

FACE: Yellow complexion; saddle like pigmentation on nose and cheeks. Rosacea.

STOMACH: Empty feeling relieved by eating; nausea at smell and sight of food or tobacco and in the morning; longing for tasty, spicy food especially vinegar; aversion to milk, salty foods and fat.

RECTUM: Constipation with sensation as if a ball were in the rectum; rectal prolapse.

FEMALE: Bearing down sensation as if everything is going to escape through the vagina—frequently crosses legs in response to this sensation of imminent protrusion; prolapsed uterus; irregular menses, too early or too late. May be of value in sterility.

BACK: Low backache, generally relieved by strenuous exercise.

SKIN: Sallow; sweats easily in axillae, back and genital region; herpes; vesicular eruptions.

Modalities
Better for exercise, pressure and after sleep. Worse for cold, after sweating and before a thunderstorm.

Relatively few 'provings' have been conducted since Hahnemann's day thus all homoeopathic *Materia Medicas* are heavily dependent on his proving descriptions. It may seem strange that information which is approximately 200 years old, as it were, is still of such fundamental importance. However, the drug pictures he compiled are as valid now as they were then, even though the descriptive language is very dated, because one can safely assume that the remedies have not altered. Most remedies are made from naturally occuring substances; refined or processed substances are rarely used. Additionally it can be presumed that people are still essentially the same.

One can, nevertheless, argue that the types of diseases from which they suffer have changed from predominately acute conditions to chronic ones and this surely necessitates new, different remedies. However, it should now be apparent that homoeopathy is not primarily interested in a specific diagnosis but in each person's highly individual reaction to the different stresses imposed on him by his environment, be they bacteriological, psychological etc. This reaction manifests as a complex range of symptoms and it is these with which homoeopathy is concerned. The similarity between the symptoms of two people suffering from the 'same disease' is usually limited to the characteristic, gross pathological signs. Beyond these the patient's symptoms do not generally have any direct association with that particular disease. Hence the situation where different remedies are prescribed for the same disease and where the same remedy is given for different diseases often arises in the practice of homoeopathy. For example, eczema which is worse for washing, heat (particularly warmth of the bed), and scratching would probably be treated with *Sulphur;* yet eczema which is worse for eating salt and being at the seaside, but better for open air and cold bathing indicates *Natrum mur.,* common salt, as the appropriate remedy. On the other hand, providing other key symptoms match, *Arsenicum album* is one of the most effective remedies in the treatment of both gastro-enteritis and asthma; two totally unrelated conditions. In other words, the gross pathology often plays a fairly minor part in determining the most suitable remedy; mental and general characteristics, plus the modalities, need to be considered. The overall symptom pictures of patients today, seen from this wider perspective, are more than adequately represented in the symptom pictures of drugs proved many, many years ago.

Hahnemann's Methods and Sources

In view of the fact that the homoeopathic *Materia Medica* derives extensively from Hahnemann's work it would be instructive to assess critically his methods and sources. It is impossible to over-emphasize the importance of the *Materia Medica* and the information contained therein, as it is intrinsic to the method of homoeopathy itself. Much attention is given to methodological details concerning which potency to use, but the reliability and accuracy of the drug pictures are seldom assessed or even questioned. It does not require much insight to realize that the practice of homoeopathy stands or falls on the quality of the information presented in the various *Materia Medicas.*

Hahnemann decided that the only reliable way of elucidating the power of a drug was to test it on healthy people and note in detail the resultant effects. Prior to this practice of 'proving' drugs on healthy people, the only ways of discovering effective medicines were those of chance and 'pseudo-rational' methods such as the 'Doctrine of Signatures'. Remedies such as Cinchona bark for malaria and Mercury for syphilis plus many others could probably be relegated to the 'accidental discovery group', and in the words of Dr Richard Hughes, a famous English Homoeopath at the turn of the century, 'theories of the *modus operandi* of such remedies have often been subsequently framed, but it is certain that their original adoption grew out of no such theories.' The 'Doctrine of Signatures' proposes the use of substances, botanical or sometimes animal, which bear a visual resemblance to the diseased part of the body. For instance, the flower of Eyebright, *Euphrasia*, is strongly suggestive of an eye and was thus used to treat eye problems. Likewise the yellow sap of the Celandine tree, *Chelidonium majus*, resembled bile and was used in bilious complaints and later extended to include liver diseases. Although this doctrine is generally regarded as a foolish fancy it has to be acknowledged that it has yielded some very effective remedies. *Euphrasia* and *Chelidonium* are but two examples which have a well-proven record in the treatment of eye and liver diseases respectively.

Hahnemann rejected the popular practice of experimenting on animals for the simple and sound reason that it was unjustifiable to extrapolate results gained in this manner to the human situation; especially in view of certain well-known illustrations of how animals and man react in totally different ways to the same substances. In Hahnemann's words:

> A pig can swallow a large quantity of *Nux vomica* without injury and yet men have been killed with fifteen grains. A dog bore an ounce of the fresh leaves, flowers and seeds of Monks hood, *(Aconite);* what man would not have died of such a dose? Horses eat it, when dried, without injury. Yew leaves, though so fatal to man fatten some of our domestic animals . . .

Additionally rabbits may feed with impunity on a diet of *Belladonna* (Deadly Nightshade) leaves! Information gained in this way would, however, be extremely valuable to that rare breed, the homoeopathic vet.

Thus the main source of knowledge of drugs must, Hahnemann concluded, be gained through the experimentation and observation of their effects on the healthy, human body. Hahnemann also examined records of poisonings and side-effects from the over-prescription of certain drugs for further information on drug action. These two sources played a fairly important part in the construction of his remedy pictures. Cases of poisoning provide particularly valuable information on the more severe and violent effects of large quantities of a drug. However, these studies are obviously limited to the relatively small class of drugs sufficiently toxic to produce such effects. Additionally it would not be practical to sit around waiting for unfortunate people to poison themselves in order to gain information on a specific drug. Well proven side-effects of different drugs also contribute to the knowledge of drug action. A certain amount of caution must be exercised for these drugs are acting on diseased bodies; some side-effects may, in fact, be the result of the disease rather than the drug. Hahnemann was well aware of this, although later on his enthusiasm for his method tended to cloud his judgement.

The Materia Medica Pura

In 1811, Hahnemann's *Materia Medica Pura* was established. It contained symptom pictures for 66 substances, all based on provings and information from poisonings and side-effects. The addition of the word *Pura* was indicative of Hahnemann's burning desire to found a *Materia Medica* which was based entirely on scientific observation and fact and was thus free of assumption.

The names of 37 people occur in connection with these particular provings, including Hahnemann himself and some members of his large family. Many of these 'provers' were young doctors who had enthusiastically embraced the homoeopathic method. They apparently formed a 'Provers' Union' so that all their experiments had legal sanction. Hahnemann, nonetheless, never abused their commendable dedication and willingness to subject themselves to a considerable amount of danger. He prepared all the medicines himself as he had a deep mistrust of the apothecaries and their practices. In fact, his outspoken opinions on this issue sent the apothecaries scurrying in the general direction of the growing anti-Hahnemann groups who, determined to protect their vested interests, were attempting to discredit both Hahnemann and his method of homoeopathy.

He first tested them on himself so that he could prescribe the appropriate strength and, with the very toxic substances, he developed suitable antidotes so that the prover could immediately allay symptoms which became too distressing. The vegetable drugs were usually administered in mother tinctures whilst other substances were given in dilutions of 1:100 or the 1c potency. The provers were then required to keep taking these small doses at specified intervals until some effect was produced. If nothing happened after a certain number of doses, Hahnemann would conclude that the prover was not sensitive enough and he was therefore no longer required to take that drug.

All provers were enjoined to avoid any extraneous influences which might distort the results. Thus he forbade the consumption of coffee, tea, wine, brandy, (but not beer of which he was very fond!), spices and strongly salted foods. He discouraged strenuous activity and exertion in case it disturbed the concentration or judgement of the prover. All provers were given diaries in which they were instructed to write down all symptoms experienced, their time of occurrence and the time of each dose. Hahnemann himself would then interrogate them on the information contained therein and attempt to filter from the vast array of symptoms the ones which could be ascribed, with confidence, to the action of the drug. This was not easy as people often react differently to the same substance.

Basically symptoms obtained from provings of this sort can be divided into two main categories: fundamental symptoms and contingent symptoms. The 'fundamental' symptoms are those which are independently reported by a fair number of the provers. These symptoms present little difficulty as their relatively high frequency of occurrence implicates the drug as the causative factor. On the other hand the 'contingent' symptoms are the result of a person's special susceptibility to that particular drug. The problem is therefore to decide whether unusual symptoms are the direct result of his individual susceptibility to the drug or whether they are spurious and belong more to the realm of imagination.

However, the clinical application of this sort of information should highlight areas of doubt and, ideally, symptoms which consistently fail, as guides to the correct remedy, should gradually be eliminated from the drug pictures.

The Provings of Chelidonium majus

The provings of *Chelidonium majus* provide an interesting example of 'fundamental' symptoms. These have been frequently verified as reliable indications for the effective use of potentized *Chelidonium*. The most widely known indication for *Chelidonium* is abdominal pain which is frequently burning, or paroxysmal, and often extends into the back. Additionally, the patients are usually better after food, particularly milk. Here are some descriptions recorded by different people who have 'proved' *Chelidonium.*

(a) 'Paroxysmal contracting of the navel.'
(b) 'Contracting sensation in the region below the stomach.'
(c) 'Violent pain in pit of the stomach as though the stomach were being constricted.'
(d) 'Constrictive sensation right across the naval as if a rope were pulled tight around the body.'
(e) 'A sharpish painful stitch right into the pit of the stomach, passing through the body and into the back.'

With reference to milk: —

(a) 'Great thirst for milk and afterwards feeling good in the whole body.'

(b) 'Milk soup which she normally did not tolerate well, was quite beneficial today.'

(c) 'Milk tastes lovely to her, better than ever.'

A great many other symptoms were obtained from the provings in addition to those described. However, two examples from the *British Homoeopathic Journal* shall now be cited, of people who benefited from potentized *Chelidonium* in order to demonstrate how artificially induced drug diseases (i.e. the drug pictures obtained from provings) often bear striking resemblances to natural disease pictures.

(1) *Mr X:* 'It is my stomach that gives me trouble. I get paroxysmal pains, more recently when my stomach is empty . . . The pain is mostly in the region of the duodenum. It extends through to the back and is quite paroxysmal.'

(2) *Miss K:* 'It's my stomach. It contracts convulsively. Today I drowned the pain in milk, it was alright then. Drowning it in milk was good for the stomach. When it hurts, it hurts to up in the back, but it radiates upwards exactly in the middle.'

More information on how to select the appropriate remedy will be given in the chapter on case-taking. However, it is important to mention at this point that it is not necessary to match a patient's symptoms with *all* of those recorded in the relevant drug picture. The ideal is obviously to match as many as possible, but it must be remembered that the drug picture represents a composite description of all the symptoms obtained from the many different people who proved the drug. Certainly none of the 'provers' would have experienced all of the symptoms represented in the drug picture; it would therefore be unreasonable to expect to match *all* of the drug symptoms with the patient's symptoms.

The Provings of Thuja occidentalis
The provings of *Thuja occidentalis* are of additional interest. Many symptoms occurred with great frequency, such as toothache; urethral itching and burning; nodules; warts; genital

sweating; copious urine and diminution of sexual desire. In addition to these 'fundamental' symptoms one prover reported the sensation of there being something 'alive' in his abdomen. Of the 25 provers, no other reported this feeling so it either represented an example of a 'contingent' symptom or it was simply incidental and had nothing to do with the action of *Thuja*. However this sensation is well recognized by some people and in the clinical situation it has been observed to be a reliable guiding symptom for the effective employment of potentized *Thuja*. It therefore deserves a place in the overall symptom picture of *Thuja*.

Chronic Diseases

In 1828, Hahnemann's *Chronic Diseases: Their Peculiar Nature and Homoeopathic Treatment* was published. In this book he introduced several completely new remedies such as *Sepia* (cuttle fish ink) and *Silica* (flint) and expanded some of the remedy pictures which had already appeared in his *Materia Medica Pura*. These new provings were not subjected to the strict, scientific standards which had characterized his former experiments.

It is worthwhile digressing here in order to describe Hahnemann's personal circumstances at this time as many authors believe they had a powerful impact on his work. In 1828 Hahnemann was 63 years old and had been living in Köthen for seven years, where, apart from working in his very busy practice, he had led a life of seclusion. This was a dramatic change from the stimulating, intellectual life of Leipzig where, prior to his enforced exile, he had been permanently surrounded by fresh, young students eager for more knowledge of homoeopathy. Strict observation and experiment had dominated his life in Leipzig, whereas his life in Köthen was characterized by a hitherto atypical inclination towards hypothesis and speculation. His concepts of *psora*, the vital force and the dynamization of the remedies all belong to this period.

Hahnemann no longer proved medicines on himself or on other healthy volunteers although some of his keener students, Dr Stapf for one, continued to do so and these results were incorporated into the drug pictures of his *Chronic Diseases*. The bulk of the information in his book was, however, obtained from the proving of potentized remedies on sick people. Thus he had relinquished the practice of proving drugs on healthy bodies, a very strange fact considering his previously earnest insistence on this, and had also adopted the notion that all remedies should be proved in the 30th potency (30c).

His new provings consisted of recording all the symptoms experienced by a sick person undergoing treatment with a particular remedy in the 30th potency. He then simply attributed all these effects to the remedy they were taking. This is totally unjustifiable and the following example well illustrates his over-credulity on this matter as well as the problems associated with proving drugs on diseased people. A woman with advanced lung cancer which had spread from the breast was receiving *Conium* (Hemlock) in potency. Not surprisingly she coughed up pus before she died (infection often accompanies advanced lung cancer) yet Hahnemann attributed the 'purulent expectoration' to the effect of *Conium*.

His sudden insistence on proving all remedies in the 30th potency is equally difficult to defend. Clearly proving remedies in their potentized form is of value in revealing the finer points of action of the drug and with substances which are far too poisonous to take in substantial amounts. In fact it is essential to do so in the provings of remedies such as *Natrum mur.* and *Silica* which have little effect in their crude state and can only reveal their valuable properties in a potentized form. Likewise other substances which have certain effects in their crude state often reveal additional properties when proved in potency.

For instance, a doctor working at the American Institute for Homoeopathy wrote, in 1868, that repeated doses of *Iris versicolor* (Blue Flag) tincture produced little but local effects whereas the 5x potency led to the development of a genuine sciatica. It will be remembered that remedies up to 12c and 24x still contain the remedy in a material form; above these potencies one is unable to detect any physical presence of the remedy. Recent attempts at the Royal London Homoeopathic Hospital to prove certain remedies in the 30th potency have met with little success. Nevertheless, evidence does seem to imply that it is possible to prove remedies in these higher potencies but only on the small category of people who are sufficiently 'sensitive'. The vast majority of healthy people remain unaffected by potentized remedies, especially as far as the higher potencies are concerned. In other words, the description of homoeopathic remedies as being harmless should be qualified in view of the fact that a small minority of people could develop some of the symptoms characteristic of the particular remedy they are taking. These would only be transitory and would disappear on stopping the remedy.

This state of affairs warrants further explanation for on the one hand potentized remedies are able to cure diseases but on the other hand they are generally incapable of producing any effects in a healthy person. The answer must lie in the subtlety of the homoeopathic method itself, for it states that only remedies selected according to the *similimum* principle will have the power to cure. Remedies chosen in this manner only affect the precise areas of the body which are out of balance or diseased. As mentioned before, there is evidence that diseased tissue is far more sensitive to various stimuli. Thus, what will affect diseased tissue may not have any effect on that same tissue when in a healthy state.

In summary, Hahnemann used four different means of assessing drug action: poisonings, side-effects in sick people resulting from over-dosage, provings on healthy bodies and the apparent effects (genuine and supposed) of potentized remedies on sick people. Clearly the provings on healthy bodies and cases of poisonings are superior to the other two sources in accuracy and reliability. His *Materia Medica Pura* drug pictures are mainly the result of provings on healthy bodies and as such should be largely reliable. His *Chronic Diseases* drug pictures are based primarily on the genuine and supposed effects of remedies on sick people and must therefore be treated with circumspection.

Clinical Symptoms

There is an additional method of contributing to the individual drug pictures; Hahnemann barely hinted at it, but his successors have seized upon the procedure with an uncritical fervour and it has become the chief way of building up drug pictures. Symptoms obtained in this way are referred to as 'clinical'

Lycopodium (Club Moss)

symptoms for the following reason. A patient presents with six
very obvious symptoms which, for argument's sake, are: great
debility accompanied by weight loss, irritability, depression,
indigestion, dysuria (pain on urinating) and acne. The first five
symptoms correspond closely to those obtained from the
provings of *Lycopodium* (club moss) and the administration of
potentized *Lycopodium* is found to remove all the symptoms,
including the acne which is unrepresented in the provings. If
another person presents with acne which disappears under the
action of *Lycopodium*, the temptation to include this symptom
in the drug picture is very strong. This is, in fact, what must have
happened to a large extent with *Lycopodium* for, because of its
low toxicity and the resultant need to prove it in potency, there
is very little information on its effects on healthy bodies. Yet
Lycopodium is one of the most commonly used remedies and it
has a very detailed drug picture. This includes a range of fairly

severe skin affections, the curious 4-8pm aggravation of symptoms etc. All of these could be classified as 'clinical' symptoms, i.e. symptoms which have been cured by potentized *Lycopodium* but are unrepresented in the provings.

There are several points concerning 'clinical' symptoms. Firstly, if they are reliable, they are invaluable as useful indications for the correct remedy. Secondly, important as they may be, they are not based on the *similimum* principle because, for instance, *Lycopodium* has never yet produced a 4-8pm aggravation in any person. However, since provings of remedies have rarely been conducted on more than fifty different people it is possible that these symptoms might be represented if the substance was proved on thousands of people. Nonetheless, until they appear in provings they should, ideally, be distinguished from 'proving' symptoms and their source and reliability indicated. Initially they were distinguished by specific signs, but this practice soon ceased altogether and clinical symptoms were extensively and uncritically incorporated into various *Materia Medicas.*

The Concept of Constitution

With one exception, the later *Materia Medicas* have simply copied this information blindly, without attempting to identify the sources. Dr Richard Hughes, the exception, was dissatisfied with this state of affairs and undertook the unenviable task of compiling a *Materia Medica* which excluded all 'clinical' symptoms and included only 'proving' symptoms which had occurred in more than one person. He also disliked the use of schemes as a method of presenting the symptoms and chose to write the prover's reports in narrative form. This is more readable than a schematic version and offers a substantially better insight into the action of the various remedies. The result of this industry was his *Cyclopedia of Drug Pathogenesy* and is perhaps the most scholarly work, since Hahnemann's *Organon*, which has been written on the subject of homoeopathy. Needless to say, it has never been recognized as such because, at the time of its publication, powerful 'winds of change' were blowing the more exciting Kentian concepts of constitution and high potency from America.

Dr James Kent and his British disciple, Dr Margaret Tyler,

each compiled a series of very influential drug pictures. In these pictures one finds statements such as tall, slim brunettes with narrow pelvises respond best to *Sepia*, *Pulsatilla* is suited to blonde women; *Sulphur* types are untidy and *Lycopodium* types prefer solitude. These symptoms definitely have no foundation in the *similium* principle (it is hard to imagine a drug changing the shape of one's pelvis) not, in fact, can they be described as 'clinical' symptoms in terms of the definition outlined previously. 'Clinical' symptoms were those which disappeared under treatment; the above descriptions refer more to genetic constitutions and personalities and as such are unlikely to alter during treatment.

There is nothing wrong with the concept that certain types of people, because of a special affinity for a particular drug, will respond very positively to it. Hahnemann himself first observed this and remarked that *Nux vomica* seemed particularly well suited to very fiery, violent people or people whose dispositions were malicious and whose tempers were easily aroused. On the other hand *Pulsatilla* was well suited to timid, anxious people, inclined to be tearful and possessing a mild, gentle and yielding disposition. Nonetheless, these few remarks are a far cry from the enormous pre-eminence given to constitutional descriptions, by a large number of homoeopathic practitioners today when selecting a remedy. In this sense one has to agree with Dr A. Campbell of the Royal London Homoeopathic Hospital, who believes we departed from the *similimum* principle seventy years ago and if we are to persist in defining homoeopathy in terms of the 'like cures like' principle, it is high time we returned to it. Unless the drug pictures are derived mainly from provings on healthy people there is nothing to distinguish homoeopathy from other methods of drug treatment, except the concept of the minimum dose which is an extension rather than a fundamental part of the method.

These are strong words, but if homoeopathy is to gain acceptance in orthodox medicine it must operate under stricter criteria. There is a vast amount of excellent and reliable material available, as Hughes' book reveals, and this should be examined and the information contained in the *Materia Medica* re-evaluated. This does not mean 'clinical' symptoms and constitutional characteristics must be excluded, as they are of great value. They should, however, be distinguished from all 'proving' symptoms.

Types of Remedy Substances

On a lighter note, the types of substances which are suitable as remedies will now be discussed. Initially, Hahnemann proved the drugs commonly employed in his day, e.g. *Arconite* (Monkshood), Cinchona bark, *Helleborus niger, Belladonna*, Arsenic etc. These substances were quite toxic and were thus easy to prove in the sense that repeated small doses were guaranteed to produce a number of effects on the healthy volunteer. However, with the development of his theory of potentization, a whole range of substances, previously considered to have no medicinal powers because they were relatively inert in their crude state, became remedy candidates, e.g. *Natrum mur., Calc. Carb.* etc. These necessarily had to be proved in a 'potentized' form in order to establish symptom pictures. In fact, on surveying the range of remedies, one is forced to conclude that there is very little which can be excluded from a homoeopathic *Materia Medica*.

Many types of substances are drawn from the three different kingdoms: animal, vegetable and mineral. Some choice examples representing the different groups will be discussed.

Vegetable

(1) *Bryonia alba:* prepared from the root of wild hops. Before Hahnemann's time it was only known as a drastic emetic and purgative and little used. It was proved originally by Hahnemann and his group and later re-proved by the Austrian Homoeopathic Society. Hahnemann said of it: 'The symptoms it excites in the healthy correspond to many affections of daily occurrence . . . and hence its healing power must be of wide range.' This is indeed the case and *Bryonia* is very commonly employed in cases of rheumatism, dyspepsia and respiratory affections, which are worse from movement and where there is an obvious dryness of mucous membranes—dry mouth; dry cough; dry, crumbling stools etc.

(2) *Coffea Cruda:* prepared from the unroasted coffee bean. Hahnemann was responsible for conducting provings with this substance and in the words of one of the provers *Coffea*

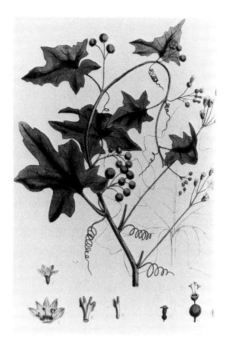

Bryonia alba

produced a, 'pathological excitation of all the organic functions.' He also described how all the organs of sense became hypersensitive to various stimuli and the well-known characteristic of sleeplessness. Thus *Coffea* is often given, in potency, when pain is felt excessively, for instance, in labour, in cases of nervous excitement and especially in insomnia where ideas keep crowding the mind.

(3) *Conium* (Hemlock): One of the most famous, if involuntary, provings of *Conium* was undoubtedly that of Socrates which was graphically described by Plato. In the words of Boericke: 'The ascending paralysis it produces, ending in death by failure of respiration, shows the ultimate tendency of many symptoms produced in the provings, for which *Conium* is an excellent remedy, such as difficult gait, trembling, sudden loss of strength while walking, painful stiffness of legs and general weakness of body and mind.'

Conium (Hemlock)

Mineral

(1) *Graphites* or *Plumbago* (the black lead of pencils). This was originally proved by Hahnemann and re-proved by several other people at a later date. Hahnemann included *Graphites* amongst his anti-psoric remedies, probably because of its remarkable healing effect on a range of skin diseases, notably eczema.

(2) *Mercury.* Mercury was a favourite drug in Hahnemann's day and it was one of the first to be proved by Hahnemann. Since it was widely and indiscriminately employed there was also plenty of information on its toxicological side-effects. Hahnemann had commented on the incredible similarity between the artificially induced mercurial fever (the result of prolonged dosing with mercury) and the condition of syphilis (which the drug was used to treat) before he had even propounded his homoeopathic principle.

Animal

(1) Snake venom, e.g. *Lachesis* (Bushmaster snake), *Crotalus horridus* (rattle snake) and *Naja tripudians* (cobra). The provings of *Lachesis* were performed by Dr Constantine Hering and several others whilst on an expedition in South America, sponsored by the King of Saxony. Hering was a colourful, exuberant character, who, in the early 1800's espoused and furthered the cause of homoeopathy with great enthusiasm. He was responsible for the introduction of several new remedies; all native to South America. The provings of *Lachesis* were understandably done in the 30th potency, but some of the symptoms recorded appeared in Dr Hering while actually preparing the different potencies. *Crotalus horridus* was proved by different people using the 1st and 2nd potencies and some of them were even dedicated enough to swallow the poison bags which had been made into pills using cheese!

(2) *Apis mellifica:* the poison of the honey bee. The use of this substance, it need hardly be said, is peculiar to homoeopathic practice. The remedy is either made from the whole bee (macerated and made into a mother tincture) or, as Hering suggests, by seizing the bee by the wings and getting it to eject its poison onto a piece of sugar. Alternatively one can carefully remove the sting and poison bags from a stupefied bee. If the poison only is used it is usually referred to as *Apis virus*. Provings of this remedy were conducted, although a lot of information was derived from the observed effects of a bee sting. When this occurs the affected part rapidly swells and becomes hot, red and painful. This is often accompanied by considerable burning, tingling and itching. It is therefore frequently employed in local affections which have the above characteristics.

Nosodes and Isopathy
Mention must be made of a particular class of remedies which are referred to as nosodes. Nosodes are either made, in the homoeopathic way, from the actual products of a disease, (e.g. pus), the diseased tissue itself or the implicated pathogenic organism. These remedies are usually administered in potencies greater than 12c which, although still 'active' are considered safe as molecules of the virulent substances are no longer present.

Here are some examples from a particular group of nosodes: *Morbillinum* (derived from a measles infection), *Parotidinum* (mumps), *Pertussin* (whooping cough), *Influenzinum* (influenza) and *Rubella* (German measles). These nosodes are sometimes given prophylactically, in other words, they are given to prevent the person from contracting the particular disease. Aside from the size of the dose, this is very similar to the practice of vaccination where, in the case of polio, specially treated forms of the polio virus are given to protect people from getting the disease. More commonly nosodes are given when the patient complains that he has never been well since he had a particular disease. For example *Parotidinum* might be given if a patient felt that he had never fully recovered from an episode of mumps.

Nosodes are rarely employed in the acute stage of the disease. As no formal provings have been conducted on those mentioned there are no symptom pictures on which to base a prescription. The only available indications for their use are therefore *prophylaxis* and the 'never been well since' syndrome. Clearly this is not homoeopathic prescribing as defined by the *similimum* principle.

The term 'isopathy' has been coined to describe the practice of treating diseases and their related conditions with substances which are identical to that of the disease itself or its causative agents. This concept has in fact been applied in orthodox medicine in the treatment of allergies with small amounts of the appropriate allergens. For example attenuated forms of certain types of pollen are given to hay fever sufferers who have a specific allergy to those types. Likewise, some homoeopathic practitioners use potencies of house dust, pollen, grasses, dog-hairs, moulds etc. to treat specific allergies. In fact any situation where side-effects or allergic reactions can be attributed to particular substances lends itself to this practice. For example, certain drug or food allergies could be treated with a potentized form of the implicated substance; potentized wheat for a wheat allergy and so forth. Results, in both the homoeopathic and orthodox fields of 'isopathic' prescribing are sufficiently promising to warrant further investigation.

There are, however, two other categories of nosodes. All of these nosodes have detailed symptom pictures which are mainly derived from 'clinical' observations rather than results obtained from provings. The first group includes the following nosodes: *Medorrhinum* (gonorrheal discharge), *Syphilinum/Lueticum* (syphilitic discharge), *Carcinosinum* (cancerous tissue), *Psorinum* (scabies vesicle) and *Tuberculinum* (tuberculosis tissue). These particular nosodes, like the others, are often used if there is a past history or even a family history (indicative of a possible susceptibility) of the disease in question. Otherwise they are chosen whenever a patient's symptom picture corresponds closely with the symptom pictures which have been ascribed to the various nosodes. They are usually included in standard homoeopathic *Materia Medica*.

The second group are referred to as 'bowel nosodes'. These remedies were originally developed by Dr Edward Bach and later by Dr John Paterson, a bacteriologist and physician working in Glasgow. They investigated the types of bacteria which predominated in a person's intestine by making stool cultures. They discovered that the presence of certain bacteria was consistently related to a specific range of disease symptoms. Since the main type of bacteria seemed to be so closely linked to the condition of the patient they began to administer potentized forms of that bacteria. They believed that this would act, like appropriate homoeopathic remedies, by finely stimulating the body's defence mechanisms. Most practitioners do not have the facilities to make bacterial cultures; bowel nosodes are therefore usually prescribed if the patient's symptoms are similar to those which were found to occur when a particular bacteria was predominant. These nosode pictures which are not based on classical proving methods have not yet found their way into homoeopathic *Materia Medicas*.

Biochemic Salts and Flower Remedies

Before this chapter is concluded, the Schüssler salts and Bach flower remedies will be briefly discussed as their relationship to homoeopathy is often clouded with confusion.

The Bach flower remedies were developed by the pathologist Dr Edward Bach who also pioneered the work on the bowel nosodes. Bach seemingly had an incredible sensitivity to the forces of nature and found that the presence of different flowers induced a certain range of emotions in him. Each flower was associated with its own unique set of emotional experiences. For example the dominant emotion of *Mimulus* was fear and that of Rock Rose, shock. Using the homoeopathic principle he would prescribe a certain remedy if its associated mental symptoms corresponded closely to those of the patient. The remedy indications are exclusively mental. Bach believed that all diseases had their origins in this sphere and treatment could only be effective if the mental symptoms were considered. The remedies are prepared in a different way from homoeopathic remedies and they are only available in a standard preparation.

On the other hand the twelve tissue salts, adopted by Dr Schüssler, are made in the same way as homoeopathic remedies although they are routinely prescribed in the 6x potency. Schüssler was initially very involved in the practice of homoeopathy but in the later part of his life he withdrew from the ranks of the homoeopaths in order to take up an independent position. He maintained that these twelve remedies were the basic constituents of the human body and the indications for their use had nothing to do with the homoeopathic principle. Schüssler's ideas were an elaboration of Dr Von Grauvogl's argument which was that an excess of any of these twelve tissue remedies in the blood could over-stimulate and thus exhaust the mechanisms by which they are absorbed. This would paradoxically lead to a state of deficiency in the tissues. He believed, however, that this state could be rectified by giving the appropriate salt in 6x potency which would act as a specific stimulus and raise the depressed vital activity to its normal state.

The twelve tissue salts are *calcium flouride, calcium phosphate, calcium sulphate, ferrum phosphate, potassium chloride, potassium phosphate, potassium sulphate, magnesium phosphate, sodium chloride, sodium phosphate, sodium sulphate* and *silica.* Each salt has detailed indications for its use and, although he maintained that they acted biochemically and had nothing to do with homoeopathy, their indications have many points of resemblance with the relevant homoeopathic drug pictures.

5. The Selection of the Similar Remedy

As previously indicated, the aim in homoeopathic prescribing is to find a remedy whose symptom picture closely resembles the total symptom picture of the patient. This suggests a simplicity which unfortunately is not apparent in practice. True parallels between the patient's complete symptom picture and drug pictures do not exist although one can often discover extraordinarily close resemblances between the two. Homoeopathic annals thus contain various different formulae which attempt to make this search for the *similimum*, the most closely matching remedy, more systematic and less haphazard. It is no wonder that the issue has become a little confused.

Striking and Uncommon Symptoms
In order to gain some clarity on this matter it is best to consult Hahnemann's writings. Hahnemann stated categorically that the patient's symptoms in their entirety must be considered when choosing an appropriate remedy. However, this view is slightly qualified by the more detailed practical advice he gave in his *Organon:*

> The more striking, singular, uncommon and peculiar signs and symptoms of the case are chiefly and most solely to be kept in view. The more general and undefined symptoms: loss of appetite, headache, debility etc. demand but little attention when of that vague and indefinite character if they cannot be more accurately described, as symptoms of such a general nature are observed in almost every disease and every drug.

This advice should form the basis of homoeopathic prescribing. Dr R. A. F. Jack, a homoeopathic general practitioner, likens the process to that used by the police when on a manhunt. Information such as: tattoo on right leg; missing index finger; scar on left cheek and so on makes their task considerably easier because the number of possible suspects is very limited. General and vague information such as: blonde hair, medium build and so on is of very limited use because so many people fit these descriptions. Likewise in homoeopathy, if a patient presents with a striking and uncommon symptom the search for a suitable remedy is much easier than if the patient presents with several ill-defined symptoms. For instance, the sensation of there being something alive in one's abdomen is only found in a few drug pictures: *Crocus*, *Sulphur* and *Thuja* for example. Thus, if a patient reports this as a prominent symptom the most suitable of these remedies would probably be prescribed. However, if a patient simply complains of nausea and cannot describe the condition in more precise terms the information is virtually useless for there are hundreds of remedies which have nausea in their symptom pictures. The homoeopathic practitioner would then have to investigate the rest of the patient's symptoms in order to find some more striking and uncommon symptoms which would be of value in indicating a suitable remedy. If, on the other hand, a patient complains of nausea which is always relieved by eating then this information is of great value for there are only a few remedies which have 'nausea relieved by eating' in their symptom pictures.

Pathological and Constitutional Prescribing

The real difficulty obviously arises if a patient's major symptoms are not collectively represented in any single drug picture. For example, one remedy may only suit his mental state, another his particular physical complaint and so on. Hahnemann taught that a single remedy should preferably be administered and thus several different approaches have been developed to deal with this problem. The Kentian school, following Hahnemann, believe in the single remedy prescription. When they are faced with the above problem, priority is given to matching the mental and then general symptoms. The more local pathological symptoms are considered to be of the least value when selecting a remedy.

This is known as 'constitutional prescribing' since the patient's temperament, his emotional state, his general reaction to his environment etc., are given precedence over the gross, pathological symptoms of his disease when selecting the most similar remedy.

On the other hand, the so-called 'pathological' school, when faced with the above problem, select a remedy which corresponds more closely to the symptoms directly associated with a particular disease rather than the mental or general symptoms of the patient.

In France and Germany, the practice of 'polypharmacy' is common; several remedies are given at a time so that most of the patient's symptoms are 'covered' in a single prescription.

Clearly, views on how to select the most similar remedy are widely divided. All schools basically agree that the totality of the patient's symptoms must be considered. However, since this is not always practicable, it is understandable that different approaches have evolved.

The Kentian homoeopaths believe that remedies selected according to the patient's constitution are deep-acting and effect a beneficial change in the body as a whole so that it becomes more effective at combating the processes of disease. However, the concept of constitution has become very confused as the term is used in different contexts to mean different things. Basically, it evolved from the observation, starting in fact from Hahnemann, that certain types of persons seemed to respond exceptionally well to certain remedies. This was greatly expanded by Kent and his followers to include characteristics such as build, colouring, appearance, mannerisms, etc. Thus, one hears of a *Sulphur* type who is supposed to be a 'stoop-shouldered', rather unkempt, red-faced, talkative, self-opinionated and warm-blooded patient. Or the tall, delicate looking, red-haired *Phosphorus* patient.

Although these descriptions may often be useful guides in selecting the remedy they are misleading for several reasons. Firstly, they do not have their origins in provings and do not therefore have anything to do with the fundamental homoeopathic principle. Secondly, they are only guides, not absolute rules. Many people have wrongly assumed that a particular remedy, in spite of a close resemblance on many points, cannot be prescribed because the patient does not conform to the constitutional type associated with that remedy. Equally, not every red-haired patient would benefit from taking *Phosphorus*.

The distinction between symptoms of health and those of disease has become clouded by this constitutional concept. For instance, jealousy is a characteristic symptom of *Lachesis*, the Bushmaster snake, and fussy tidiness of *Arsenicum album*. Does this mean that *Lachesis* should only be prescribed when the person is uncharacteristically jealous or *Arsen. alb.* when the person is unusually fastidious? Or should *Lachesis* or *Arsen. alb.* be prescribed even if jealously or fastidiousness has always been an integral part of their 'healthy' nature? Again, it is worthwhile consulting Hahnemann's writings for some clarification. From these it seems fairly obvious that the most important symptoms are those which represent a change from the normal, especially in the mental sphere. For example, sudden irritability, weepiness or jealousy. These are symptoms on which to base a prescription.

Hahnemann did not differentiate between diseases of the body and diseases of the mind. In fact he stated that mental diseases were simply 'corporeal diseases in which the symptoms of derangement of the mind had become predominant.' Since medicines are capable of changing a person's disposition (for instance, gold can induce a state of severe depression) it is important to carefully note the person's disposition as this could be a crucial factor in determining the appropriate remedy.

Hahnemann regarded symptoms as indicative of underlying disease processes. The aim in prescribing the similar remedy is therefore to remove these particular symptoms by restoring health and harmony to the body. Clearly all symptoms which represent a change from normal reflect these underlying disease processes. Many of the constitutional symptoms such as build, colour etc. are not symptoms of disease and as such will not be altered in any way by the similar remedy. In conclusion it would be ideal if, for the sake of clarity, information regarding the types of person who should respond well to particular remedies was clearly distinguished from information, particularly as regards the mental symptoms, which has been acquired through provings.

It should also be mentioned that Kent, who was largely responsible for the constitutional remedy indications, was, in fact, guilty of contradiction. He categorically stated in his writings, 'the morbid condition of body or mind, or both, is composed of signs and symptoms not belonging to the health of the patient, no matter how recent or long standing they may be.' Additionally, he wrote that temperaments which were natural demanded no consideration as they could not be changed in any manner by homoeopathic remedies. In fact, he stated very firmly that twisting temperaments which were not based on provings into the drug symptom pictures was but a misunderstanding of homoeopathic principles. From these writings, ironically enough, it would seem that he was in total accord with the idea that it is the change from the normal, the result of 'morbid' processes, which is of utmost importance in the selection of a remedy.

Taking a Homoeopathic Case History
In taking a homoeopathic history, it is best to list all the main symptoms with their particular modalities, taking particular note of striking and uncommon ones. Careful and sensitive questioning is of utmost importance, as accurate information is essential. Although the practitioner must obviously direct the questioning, the patient's answers should be voluntary, spontaneous and free of suggestion. This is critical for it is often tempting to get the patient to be more specific about a certain complaint than he can possibly be. In Hahnemann's terms, if the symptom is vague and ill-defined, especially to the patient, then it should not be an important consideration in the choice of the remedy. For instance, when a person volunteers the information that his headache always seems to be worse for movement one can consider that as a striking and obvious symptom. However, when a person who suffers from headaches only agrees that it might be worse on movement after persistent questioning, this fact is not useful and should not be used as an important factor in determining the appropriate remedy.

The information contained in the homoeopathic *Materia Medica* is of such a detailed and varied nature that case-taking must necessarily involve recording details of all aspects of a patient. Some examples will be given of the types of enquiries a homoeopathic practitioner should make and how facts gained in this way can often immediately suggest a particular remedy.

The history of the patient's particular complaint or complaints must be taken. Circumstances of events strongly associated with the start of the complaint can suggest specific remedies. For instance, *Arnica* would probably be given if the complaint was associated with a particular injury. *Thuja*, which is known to be a good vaccination antidote, might be given if the start of a particular complaint could be traced to a vaccination. *Ignatia* might be suitable if the patient had been adversely affected by the loss of a loved one.

As mentioned before, the practice of prescribing nosodes has become increasingly common. For instance, the use of *Morbillinum* if the patient had never been well since a bout of measles, or *Carcinosinum* if there is a family history of cancer. Thus, enquiries of this nature will probably be made by the homoeopathic practitioner.

The modalities and precipitating factors, if any, of particular symptoms must be ascertained. Whether a symptom is better or worse for heat, pressure, movement, cold, food, a particular time of day or year and so on, can provide vital information in the selection of the correct remedy.

In addition to recording details of the patient's complaints, questions concerning all other bodily parts and functions should be asked. Thus one should enquire about symptoms related to the head, eyes, ears, nose, throat, face, mouth, respiratory system, stomach, abdomen, rectum, genito-urinary system, back, extremities and skin. This is of vital importance for details gained in these areas, although they may be of no real significance to the patient, can often indicate the correct remedy.

In the sphere of mental symptoms specific enquiries about worries can reveal much valuable information. 'The dread of having an incurable disease' might suggest *Lilium tigrinum* or the fear which precedes an exam or interview could well indicate *Argentum nitricum*. Likewise, enquiries about a person's temper might reveal that the patient has periodic outbursts of 'violent passion'. This almost certainly would point to

Staphisagria, unless the patient's other symptoms totally contra-indicated this remedy.

General reactions to the physical environment such as heat, cold, damp, wind, thunder, sun, weather changes, the sea etc. must be noted. For instance, *Pulsatilla* might be suitable if the person positively disliked hot weather and found stuffy, hot atmospheres particularly oppressive. On the other hand people who feel worse during a thunderstorm could suggest *Phosphorus* as the correct remedy.

Information about the patient's appetite and food preferences is useful as long as it is not the result of religious beliefs, dietary habits or advice. Food preferences which are completely genuine should only be considered. For example, a strong craving for salt could indicate *Natrum muriaticum.* If a patient were to have an unnatural craving for indigestible things like chalk, coal or pencils as well as an aversion to fatty foods then *Calcarea carbonica* should be considered. Several remedies, mainly *Sulphur* and *Phosphorus,* show a strong mid-morning hunger sensation.

Details regarding when and where the patient perspires, as well as the type of odour, if any, can be useful. Nightly head-sweating which is sufficient to soak the pillow is a very characteristic symptom of *Calcarea carbonica.* Putrid smelling sweat and other secretions such as breath, stools, and urine strongly suggest *Baptisia.*

Sleeping patterns and habits can provide positive remedy indications. People who wake at 3 a.m. and cannot sleep again until near morning and thus awaken feeling wretched points to *Nux vomica.* Sleeping with hands above one's head is a very typical *Pulsatilla* symptom. In addition, significant and recurrent dreams, whether of snakes, fires, escaping, falling or dying can well be indicative of a specific remedy.

Modalities, especially if unusual, can often point to a particular remedy. These generally refer to factors which make the symptom better or worse but can also refer to the person as a whole. The striking modality of *Conium* is that the symptoms are relieved by letting the limbs hang down. Very few remedies are characterized by this modality.

Hahnemann grouped all the symptoms characteristic of different remedies into the various schemes: mind, head, eye, etc. He therefore instructed patients' symptoms to be similarly grouped so that an easy comparison between drug pictures and a patient's symptom picture could be made. This was feasible in the early history of the homoeopathic method for there were less than a hundred remedies in a homoeopathic *Materia Medica*. Now there are over two thousand and it would be absurd to have to compare the patient's disease picture with each one of these remedies until a close correspondence is found. The task may not be so daunting for practitioners who have acquired an extensive knowledge of the different remedies; they can often select a remedy without even referring to the *Materia Medica*. However, to the newcomer the prospect of finding the *similimum* unaided is very disheartening indeed.

Several methods of finding one's way about the *Materia Medica* have fortunately been developed. The chief one today involves the use of a Repertory which is basically an index of all the symptoms found in a *Materia Medica* along with a list of the various remedies which are associated with each symptom. These symptoms are distributed into four main sections: 'Mentals', 'Generals', 'Particulars' (relating to specific parts of the body) and 'Modalities.' Each of these contains a very wide range of descriptions. For instance, if the patient has a greasy, shiny complexion, one would look under the section entitled 'Face' which in turn includes a sub-section on the appearance or condition. Here one finds descriptions ranging from a bloated and puffy look to a dull and stupid expression as well as a greasy and shiny complexion. Under this particular symptom several remedies are listed, the most important being: *Natrum mur.* and *Plumbum.*

The Repertorial Point System

All Repertories have some sort of system for indicating the most important remedies in each list. In Kent's Repertory the most important remedies are in heavy black type, the less important ones in italics and the least important ones in ordinary type. If the remedy is in heavy black type it is assigned a value of 3 points, 2 points if in italics and 1 point if in ordinary type.

These different descriptive symptom categories are referred to as 'rubrics.' When repertorizing a patient, one lists all the main symptoms and modalities and then attempts to find appropriate rubrics, noting all the remedies associated with each of them, as in the above example. The object, once this is completed, is to try to find the remedy which is common to the greatest number of rubrics. This is not as simple as it sounds and the point system attempts to make the selection process easier. Each time the remedy appears it is worth 3, 2 or 1 point. The remedy with the largest number of points is considered to be the most appropriate remedy for the patient.

Disadvantages of Repertorization
This method is of great value to people who are unfamiliar with the various remedies. However, it suffers from several disadvantages. Firstly, it is a time consuming process. Because most Repertories were compiled in the early nineteenth century, the descriptive language is rather outdated, and much time can be spent trying to find a suitable rubric. Although the rubrics are set out in a fairly logical order they are not generally in alphabetical order. This means that one has to become familiar with the compiler's logic in order to understand his particular method of classification.

Secondly, it is no substitute for knowing and being well aware of the characteristic symptoms of the different remedies. Even Kent, a great advocator of repertorial methods, conceded this point when, on reading the case-notes of a particular patient, immediately chose *Thuja* as the appropriate remedy. This stunned his students who had been up all night repertorizing the same case and had come up with a different remedy. In response to their query he merely assured them that the patient had a discharge which was unmistakeably typical of *Thuja*. This familiarity can only be acquired with experience and astute observation.

Keynote System
Another system involves the use of 'keynotes'. These consist of a series of characteristic and striking symptoms which immediately suggest a particular remedy. If a patient presents with any of these symptoms the indicated remedy is then checked for any similarity with the rest of the patient's symptoms. If there are some further points of resemblance between the patient's symptoms and the drug effects then that

remedy will probably be prescribed.

Some books simply list a number of possible remedies for certain ailments with some of their main characteristics. For instance, under an acute headache section one would probably find *Belladonna, Bryonia, Gelsemium, Glonoine,* and *Iris versicolor.* The *Belladonna* headache is throbbing and worse on stooping, lying and noise. The face is flushed, the eyes dilated and the patient is excited and probably feverish. Under *Glonoine,* however, one would find that the headache is bursting and often brought on by exposure to the sun. The head feels very heavy but the person is unable to lay it on a pillow. Any heat around the head is intolerable. The headache of *Iris versicolor* is usually frontal with a feeling of constriction. Nausea and vomiting often accompany the headache which can be the result of mental strain. It is better for motion and worse at rest. Thus one should be able to find a description under such a heading which bears a resemblance to the type of headache one has.

Some similarity between the drug picture and the disease picture must obviously exist if the drug is to act homoeopathically. As discussed previously, the matter of the degree and type of resemblance required has led to the development of widely diverging opinions. It is perhaps worthwhile repeating Hahnemann's instructions. 'The more striking, singular, uncommon and peculiar signs and symptoms of the case are chiefly and most to be kept in view.'

Kentian homoeopaths believe and regularly state that the primary resemblance must be in the mental sphere, with pathological symptoms being of the lowest value in the search for the *similimum.* However, Kent wrote that from whatever group, mentals, generals or particulars, one must take the rare and peculiar symptoms and look for a remedy which includes these as well as covering the rest of the patient if possible. It therefore seems fair to say that this instruction is the best and most useful advice to offer in connection with the search for the *similimum.* There is also a general consensus that it is preferable to find a remedy which has at least three major symptoms in common with the patient's disease picture.

Selection of The Appropriate Potency

There are also widely diverging opinions on what potency should be used and when. Kentian homoeopaths theoretically favour the very high potencies—200c, 1M, 10M and CM— which they like to administer in a single dose. A second dose of the same or different remedy is then only prescribed when the effect of the initial dose is exhausted. Other doctors routinely employ the lower potencies and give several doses over a relatively short period of time. Hahnemann, in fact, never made or employed potencies above the 30th centesimal one. However, until such time as clinical research throws some light on the potency issue, the choice and mode of administration must remain in the realm of individual preference and experience. Perhaps a good guiding rule is to use fewer doses of the higher potencies if there is a good resemblance between the remedy and disease picture, and rather more frequent doses of the lower potencies if there is not such a high degree of similarity.

Both the high potency and the low potency prescribers strangely enough seem to achieve equally good results. One is forced to conclude that there is value in both approaches and that a lot depends on the individual patient and his unique way of reacting to various stimuli. Both sides could therefore benefit from a more flexible attitude and a willingness to experiment with the whole range of potencies. The late Dr Margery Blackie, homoeopathic physician to the Queen and Dean of the Homoeopathic Faculty, once said that after many years of experience she was convinced that there was value in both types and methods of prescribing. This was a salutary statement from a remarkable woman and a refreshing change from her earlier pleadings with the erring low potency 'pathological' prescribers to give up their evil ways and adopt the method of high potency, constitutional prescribing.

A few rather brief remedy descriptions are given in the final chapter. So that people may experiment with the method, suggestions as to the potency and frequency of the dose will be given. It must be remembered that these are only suggestions; they could not be anything else in view of the lack of agreement on the subject.

In acute diseases the remedy stimulus should be repeated

frequently and a powder, tablet or roughly ten granules should be given every 2-4 hours until relief is obtained. It must be remembered that the size of the dose seems to be relatively unimportant, it is the specific type of stimulus and the repetition of this stimulus which are crucial. It is generally considered that one tablet, one powder or a few granules represent an adequate stimulus. Taking more than this or even less does not appear to alter the overall effect of the remedy. For this reason the same dose is given to infants and adults alike.

In chronic diseases the remedy is not usually given as frequently and it is generally accepted that once improvement is initiated the person should stop taking the remedy until the effect has worn off. The same remedy can then be repeated if the patient suffers a relapse or ceases to improve any further. Sometimes the symptoms can change, in which case, a different remedy may be required. If, after several doses of a remedy there is no change to report, either the remedy must be altered or, if it obviously suits the patient's symptoms, a different potency should be tried. When assessing the effect of the remedy the reaction of the whole body must be considered.

A remedy may frequently improve the patient's sense of well-being and outlook without apparently affecting his or her particular complaint. Relief of the actual complaint may follow or a different remedy may be required.

Unfortunately, this all sounds a little vague, but it is unavoidable in view of the lack of understanding as to how homoeopathic remedies actually work. All we really know is that they can produce a series of effects ranging from the satisfactory to the miraculous.

The Homoeopathic Aggravation
Mention must be made of what has come to be known as the 'homoeopathic aggravation.' By treating likes with likes one is not counteracting, but stimulating the processes of disease which are occurring in the body. It is therefore not surprising that in some cases symptoms are made worse. In fact this phenomenon actually encouraged Hahnemann to dilute the drugs to an extent where he hoped that aggravations would disappear. However, in spite of using dilutions hitherto unconceived by the apothecaries it soon became apparent that a

very small percentage of the population were so sensitive that the high potencies could still cause aggravations. This is generally accepted to be a good sign and, more often that not, eventually results in a substantial improvement after stopping the remedy. It is therefore best to stop taking the remedy if this occurs and wait and see what develops. If the symptoms worsen whenever one attempts to resume the treatment it is advisable to change the potency or sometimes even the remedy. These aggravations are not serious but can cause concern so it is just as well to be aware of their existence.

Issues relating to the methods of remedy selection and the appropriate potency are all peripheral to the central homoeopathic maxim which simply states that likes should be treated with likes. Thus it is with this clear instruction that this chapter shall be concluded rather than the hazy and sometimes contentious rules and procedures which have grown around it.

6. Clinical Evidence in Support of Homoeopathy

Testimonies from homoeopathic practitioners and patients as to the efficacy of the homoeopathic method are inadequate as evidence that it really works. If homoeopathy is to become a widely accepted practice it must subject itself to the rigorous scientific trials which now precede the launching of all new orthodox drugs.

The ultimate assessment is the 'Double Blind Trial' which has been developed in order to diminish the bias given to results because of the 'physician' and 'placebo' effect. For instance, many studies show that the physician is frequently a powerful therapeutic agent in his own right because of the conviction he may have in his particular treatment, as well as other reasons. Other studies conclude that about 30 per cent of the population are 'placebo' responders, that is they experience relief on taking pills although, unbeknown to them, they contain no active ingredients. In a Double Blind Trial it is usual for a third party, who sees neither the physician nor the patient, to decide who will receive the active ingredient and who will receive the placebo. The two substances are made to look identical and both the physician and the patient are ignorant of what they are administering and receiving respectively.

Unfortunately there are a few problems unique to the method of homoeopathy which make the use of Double Blind Trials problematical. In orthodox trials one or two specific drugs are usually tested on a certain range of disorders. The results of such trials enable one to conclude which drug is the most effective in certain conditions. However, intrinsic to the method of homoeopathic prescribing is the requirement of strict individualization. The totality of the patient's symptoms must be considered when selecting the appropriate remedy, or *similimum*, hence it is not unusual for, say, five different remedies to be chosen for five people diagnosed as suffering from the same disease. Fortunately, this problem in a Double Blind Trial situation is not insurmountable, as a recent study in Glasgow proved.

There is a further problem which highlights the vulnerability of the homoeopathic method when examined under such harsh spotlights. The homoeopathic maxim, that of treating 'likes with likes' is only a guiding principle or rule not an inviolable law. The principle has, nonetheless, led to the selection of effective remedies often enough to warrant a place in the therapeutic field. However, since true, invariable parallels between natural disease and artificially induced drug diseases do not exist there is no simple framework in which to assess the validity of the homoeopathic principle.

In other words judgements have to be made as to what is the most similar remedy, and it is by no means uncommon for homoeopathic practitioners to select different remedies for the same person. Case-taking is a subjective affair and the information and criteria on which the remedy is selected will inevitably reflect the differences between the attitudes and beliefs of the homoeopathic practitioners. Most practitioners will admit that they frequently have to prescribe several different remedies before they 'hit' on the one which has the desired effect. Thus if, in a clinical trial situation, the patients experience no relief one cannot simply conclude that the homoeopathic principle is invalid; the remedies or even the potency may have been inappropriate.

Homoeopathy is the outsider and is therefore at a disadvantage. It is useful to remember, before one rashly judges the method, that there are many situations where allopathic prescribing has been ineffective yet these examples do not threaten or undermine the credibility of the allopathic method in general.

Historical Evidence of the Success of Homoeopathy

Before recent clinical studies are discussed, some historical evidence of the success of homoeopathy will be presented. This information does not satisfy today's high standards but is worth mentioning for several reasons. Epidemics of infectious disease provided unique opportunities to test the effectiveness of homoeopathic remedies on a large scale. The brightest page in the homoeopathic records book is, without doubt, the one concerning its success in the treatment of cholera. In fact, the success homoeopathy enjoyed in various epidemics of diseases was largely responsible for its rapid acceptance by the multitude, doctors and lay people alike, who witnessed or benefited from the effective treatment. In addition the need for strict individualization is not so apparent in acute infectious diseases and even Hahnemann remarked: 'because they arise from a contagious principle that always remains the same they also retain the same character and pursue the same course . . .' This meant that it was possible to treat most of the people with one of a small number of suitable homoeopathic remedies. It therefore became a lot easier to employ homoeopathic treatment on a large scale.

In 1831, amid widespread panic and despair, cholera reached epidemic proportions throughout the whole of Western Europe. This disease is characterized by violent diarrhoea, vomiting and cramps. The death rate is very high, mainly as a result of severe dehydration. Before Hahnemann had actually seen a case he was able to recommend several remedies on the basis of symptom reports given to him by his great nephew who was practising in St Petersburg. He suggested that *Camphor* should be used prophylactically and in the early stages, followed in later stages by one or more of the following remedies, depending on individual symptoms: *Copper, Veratrum album, Bryonia* and *Rhus toxicodendron.* It is interesting to note here that subsequent studies showed that people who had been working with copper had an apparent immunity to cholera. He also stressed the importance of proper hygiene.

The treatment proved to be remarkably successful. From Russia, Germany and Hungary in 1831-2, from Vienna in 1836, from Liverpool and Edinburgh, France and America in 1849, from London in 1854 and again from Liverpool in 1866 the evidence testified to the superiority of homoeopathic treatment. The death rate for the latter rarely exceeded 30 per cent while the death rate in orthodox hospitals was always in excess of 50 per cent.

The figure reported from Vienna was of particular significance for in 1836 the royal decree forbidding the practice of homoeopathy was still in operation. However, when it was brought to the attention of the Minister of the Interior that only one third of the cases treated by Dr Fleischmann, a homoeopathic physician, died while more than two thirds died under orthodox treatment, the law against homoeopathy was repealed.

When the cholera epidemic visited London in 1854 the mortality rate at the Royal London Homoeopathic Hospital was 16.4 per cent while the average mortality in orthodox hospitals was 51.8 per cent. The Government Inspector Dr MacLoughlin, who was a member of the orthodox establishment, testified 'most handsomely' in parliament to the severity of the cases treated in the homoeopathic hospital and to the astonishing success of the treatment. He was reputed to have ended by saying: 'If it should please the Lord to visit me with cholera I would wish to fall into the hands of a homoeopathic physician.'

Unfortunately homoeopathy was denied the full credit and recognition which is deserved. This was due to the fact that most of the results in the homoeopathic hospitals were deemed to be unreliable because they had not been supervised by the medical establishment of the day. Hahnemann himself fuelled the fire of prejudice by writing articles on cholera which included critical and abusive remarks about the medical profession and their particular treatment of cholera.

Hahnemann was certainly justified in his condemnation of the orthodox treatments for cholera. Bleeding the patient was a principal weapon despite the fact that some were so severely dehydrated that no blood flowed from their cut veins. Finding the blood dark and as 'thick as tar' only incited them to further bleedings in an effort to 'thin' the blood. Against the back-drop of this treatment which was almost certainly guaranteed to hasten the patient's death, it is tempting to simply attribute the superior homoeopathic results to the effects of the natural healing powers of the body when left alone. This may well be the case for other diseases but not for cholera which, if left alone, more often than not, ends in death through dehydration. Even today the main treatment is simple intravenous rehydration. Thus, the remarkable results achieved by the homoeopathic practitioners should be considered as a sound record of the effectiveness of homoeopathic remedies.

A recent study by Dr P. A. Ustianowski (1974) clearly demonstrated that the placebo response could not be used as the total explanation of the apparent effectiveness of homoeopathic treatment. Out of a sample of 200 women, all of whom had cystitis (bladder infection), 50 per cent received a course of placebos and the other 50 per cent received a course of *Staphisagria* 30c (wild delphinium). Of the women who received the remedy, 90 per cent had lost all relevant symptoms within a month, 8 per cent felt much better and 2 per cent were unchanged. Of the women who received the placebo, 40 per cent lost all their symptoms within a month, 10 per cent were much better and 50 per cent were unchanged.

Rheumatoid Arthritis—A Double Blind Trial

Dr Robin Gibson et al, working at the Glasgow Homoeopathic Hospital, constructed a double blind clinical trial in order to test the efficacy of homoeopathy in the treatment of rheumatoid arthritis. This trial also took into account the homoeopathic requirement for strict individualization when choosing a remedy.

Rheumatoid arthritis is a form of arthritis which affects the joints as well as other parts of the body. It is often characterized by remissions but generally runs a progressive course over many years. A large number of well controlled therapeutic trials have been carried out in this field and it therefore represented a very challenging area in which to test the potential of homoeopathy.

A total of 46 patients took part in the trial, all of whom satisfied the same criteria for 'definite' rheumatoid arthritis. Remedies were selected for each patient on the basis of his full symptomatology, according to homoeopathic principles. An independent third party then decided who would receive a course of the selected remedy and who would receive a course of the placebo; neither the physician nor the patient knew the result of the decision. No change was made in the patients' orthodox anti-inflammatory therapy as this would have introduced too many complications. All patients were seen regularly during the three month period of the trial and any changes were assessed subjectively and objectively (e.g. grip strength, limbering up time etc). After three months the patients who had been receiving a placebo were given a course of their previously selected homoeopathic remedy. There was no point in giving the homoeopathic treatment group a course of placebos as homoeopathic remedies can often continue to have an effect long after they are taken.

Significant improvements in the 'remedy' group were obtained in all the parameters which were assessed. There were no significant changes in the placebo group. Two members of this group deteriorated to such an extent that they required hospitalization, despite the fact that they were still taking their anti-inflammatory drugs. Two others dropped out and the remaining nineteen began their three month course of homoeopathic remedies. At the end of three months they experienced improvements of a similar order to the first group.

These results demonstrate clearly that homoeopathy, added to first-line anti-inflammatory therapy, is superior to placebos added to the same therapy. The improvements obtained under homoeopathic treatment compared very favourably with the results of orthodox treatments (gold, levamisole etc.). This is important in view of the fact that more than one third of patients receiving gold or levamisole treatment for example reported toxic side-effects. No side-effects were experienced by any of the patients who underwent homoeopathic treatment.

This trial is an important landmark for homoeopathy as it is the first of its kind and fulfils the rigid criteria laid down for drug assessment. It will hopefully herald a new era in the evaluation of homoeopathy. The results were certainly encouraging and should stimulate the conducting of further trials. This is necessary, for without evidence from trials of this quality, the likelihood of homoeopathy being recognized as a valid therapeutic method is very small indeed.

7. The Inadvertent Use of Homoeopathy in Orthodox Medicine

Many medicines today, which have a firm place in the armoury of 'allopathic' drugs, have their origins in herbal folklore. For example Quinine, Digitalis, *Colchicine* and *Emetine* all derive respectively from the following plants: Cinchona bark, Foxglove, Autumn Crocus *(Colchicum)* and Ipecacuanha. They are presumed to work allopathically, in other words by producing effects which are antagonistic or different from the disease process. However, Hahnemann's experiment with the Cinchona bark which led him to develop a range of symptoms accurately mimicking those of malaria (the disease the bark was used to treat) suggested the intriguing possibility that many other commonly used 'allopathic' drugs could in fact be described as homoeopathic. It is important to remember that it is the administration of a remedy which is capable of producing symptoms similar to those observed in the patient that distinguishes a treatment as homoeopathic, not necessarily the strength of the dose.

The purpose of this chapter is to explore whether some 'allopathic' drugs and practices could in fact be based and thus work on the homoeopathic principle.

Quinine, still an important drug in the treatment of malaria, is of further interest for the actual mechanism of its curative effect is still unknown. Although Quinine is capable of killing malarial parasites *in vitro* (i.e. in the laboratory situation) the concentrations of Quinine achieved in the blood reach only 1 per cent of the concentration required to kill them. This could be construed as further evidence that the action is homoeopathic and that the Quinine stimulates the host defence mechanisms rather than directly harming the parasites.

Toxicological studies of Digitalis (details of the side-effects experienced on ingesting large amounts of the drug) more than testify to its ability to induce heart failure, yet it is one of the most important allopathic drugs in the treatment of heart failure. Needless to say, homoeopathic practitioners often prescribe Digitalis, in potency, in conditions of heart failure, etc. with good results.

Colchicum, the Autumn Crocus, has been in use since the sixth century for the treatment of joint pain. *Colchicine*, a derivative, is one of the many available treatments for gout. Yet 'provings' of *Colchicum* (i.e. the effects of large amounts of *Colchicum* on healthy people) show that it is capable of inducing many acute arthritic symptoms which are similar to those experienced by the sufferer of gout.

The symptom picture obtained from 'provings' of the plant *Ipecacuanha* is briefly as follows: persistent nausea and vomiting constriction of the chest, violent and suffocative coughing with much phlegm which is difficult to expectorate, hoarseness or complete loss of voice *(aphonia)* and a range of dysenteric-type symptoms. Allopathic medicine utilizes the powerful emetic effect of *Ipecacuanha* when given in large doses in the treatment of poisoning. However, smaller doses are recommended in the treatment of children suffering from croup and whooping cough and in situations where the patient is full of phlegm which does not yield to coughing. This seems to constitute an obvious example of homoeopathic prescribing. Many cases, in homoeopathy, where patients have presented with asthma which is accompanied by nausea and vomiting have been treated with *Ipecacuanha*, in potency, to great effect. Furthermore in conventional medicine *Emetine*, a derivative of *Ipecacuanha*, is sometimes used to treat amoebic dysentery. *Ipecacuanha*, in potency, can also be effective in curing cases of amoebic dysentery.

There are further examples of allopathic treatment, for which there are no entirely satisfactory mechanistic explanations, which could represent examples of the inadvertent use of the homoeopathic principle.

In the conventional treatment of certain conditions, such as cancer, X-rays and Radium are employed, yet both of these treatments have been implicated in the cause of some cancers.

Hyperactive children are treated, not with sedatives or tranquillizers as would be expected, but with amphetamine-like drugs which are usually employed in situations where a stimulant is required.

Ergotamines, derived from the fungus which grows on Rye, are the most widely prescribed drugs in the treatment of migraine yet they induce migraine-type headaches when taken in excess.

Flouride is known to reduce the overall incidence of tooth decay. However, amongst the recorded toxic effects of taking considerable amounts of calcium flouride and fluoric acid are a rapid development of caries and defects in the tooth enamel.

Gold injections, in the form of *sodium aurothiomalate,* are frequently given to people suffering from rheumatoid arthritis, although little is understood of their action. In Britain the injections are normally given in doses of up to 50mg monthly, with varying degrees of relief, although at least 30 per cent of the patients suffer side-effects. On the Continent the pattern is different as the gold is usually administered in 1mg doses, that is as much as fifty times less than those employed in Britain. Interestingly enough, their overall results compare very favourably with the British ones, yet their patients suffer far fewer side-effects because of the use of smaller doses. It is possible that the curative action of the gold could be homoeopathic as 'provings' of gold describe a range of arthritic symptoms, particularly swollen, painful, almost ankylosed (fused) joints. Suicidal, hysterical depression also features strongly in the 'provings' of gold. It would therefore be of great interest to see whether or not those patients who respond very well to the therapy also suffer from depression. In homoeopathic terms, the more the patient's symptoms match the drug 'picture', which is obtained from the 'provings', the greater the likelihood of effecting a cure.

Clinical trials which aim to assess the performance of various orthodox drugs unfortunately deal mainly in statistics. They do not take into account, in any significant way, the individual variation in the response to the same drug. Although all patients may be suffering from a 'similar' syndrome, some will respond exceptionally well, some will only respond in a limited way and others may not respond at all. In an ideal situation it would be extremely valuable to establish beforehand whether or not any of the drugs to be tested could possibly have an underlying homoeopathic base. If so, individual variation could they be constructively assessed and used to formulate a more detailed and accurate set of criteria for the prescription of a particular drug. Additionally, all patients would suffer fewer side-effects because smaller doses could be used if the action were established as homoeopathic. It needs little imagination to see how this could revolutionize drug testing and indeed drug therapy, two areas which are very much in need of a critical assessment.

8. Why Homoeopathy Declined in Popularity

With good reason it is often asked why, if homoeopathy is so effective, has it not become part of the fabric of orthodox medical treatment? The purpose of this chapter is therefore to attempt to explain the current situation of homoeopathy with regard to the medical establishment. Since its inception this gentle, safe and successful treatment has been the target of vicious outbursts of persecutional fury and hysteria; the main culprits being doctors. Yet despite its turbulent 'career', homoeopathy has managed to weather these storms and is, in fact, in the process of reasserting itself today.

Disillusionment, primarily with orthodox drug treatment, has made people seek safe yet effective alternatives, and homoeopathy satisfies both of these criteria. In this respect it is interesting to note that people, doctors and patients alike, who have seriously tested homoeopathic remedies rarely reject them in favour of orthodox drugs. This fact, in conjunction with the persistence of the method through almost 200 years, implies that it has nothing to do with 'quackery' and those sensational 'panaceas' which periodically burst on to the scene, soon to be forgotten for ever more.

Initially the spread of the homoeopathic method was rapid, mainly because it proved to be so effective in treating acute infectious disorders. Homoeopathic practitioners quickly made a name for themselves during the various epidemics of cholera, typhoid and scarlet fever and their particular method received

wide attention and publicity. In Raab, Hungary, a homoeopathic practitioner, Dr Bakody, obtained such good results that
the inhabitants sent an appeal to their local newspaper
requesting more homoeopathic doctors to wage war against the
'dreaded foe'. Needless to say, it was never published as it was
censored by an important member of the medical establishment.

The Situation in America

In America homoeopathy was adopted by an unprecedented
number of people. It was introduced in the 1820's by a Danish
physician, Hans Gram. However, Dr Constantine Hering,
because of his indefatigable energy and enthusiasm, is
considered to be the principal architect of homoeopathy in
America. The successful employment of homoeopathic
remedies in the treatment of yellow fever, then endemic in the
southern states, also helped to establish it as a viable therapeutic
method. By 1900 no fewer than 20 per cent of all physicians in
the U.S.A. practised homoeopathy. In addition, there were 22
homoeopathic medical colleges and over 100 homoeopathic
hospitals in existence.

It has been estimated that by the turn of the century more than
400 million people were receiving homoeopathic treatment.
These remarkable statistics demand an explanation for if so
many people had chosen homoeopathy as their preferred
method of treatment, why did the medical establishment persist
in ignoring it? Even today homoeopathy is no closer to being
integrated into the structure of orthodox treatment.

Prejudice and the Drug Revolution

Two main reasons shall be advanced in explanation of this
anomaly: prejudice and the drug revolution. The history of
homoeopathy abounds with examples illustrating the prejudice
of medical men against a new method. In the eighteenth and
early nineteenth century medical practices had become
entrenched in tradition and the cherished methods of bleeding
the patient and using strong purgatives and emetics etc. had
been practised for so long that they were considered to be
inviolable. Hahnemann was alone in his condemnation of
bleeding and such was their inflexibility on this issue that Dr
Brossais (1722-1838), nicknamed the 'medical Robespierre'

because of his mania for blood-letting, was respected and popular whereas Hahnemann was ridiculed and scorned. When their methods of treatment were 'threatened', as they saw it, by the homoeopathic method, a fierce loyalty which precluded tolerance was excited. Some examples of the ways in which this intolerance was vented over the years will be described. Although it is not as obvious today, prejudice still operates but under a much more subtle guise.

In 1820 Hahnemann was 65 and had a practice in Leipzig which was becoming more and more celebrated. People were being converted to the new method daily and the fervour of the public contest between the merits of homoeopathy and those of allopathy increased as the number of converts grew. The medical establishment and the apothecaries were on one side; Hahnemann and his adherents on the other. The members of the public adopted one side or the other, and beer houses, homes and places of work resounded with the arguments for and against the two methods.

In February 1820 the apothecaries took Hahnemann to court for making and dispensing his own medicines; a practice which was illegal at that time. Hahnemann based his defence on the fact that the apothecaries charged fees according to the weight of ingredients in the prescription hence they would be unable to earn a living making homoeopathic remedies which contain an almost negligible amount of the remedy. He lost, and was forbidden to make and dispense medicines, pending confirmation later that year by the State authorities.

Prince Karl Schwarzenberg of Austria then decided to consult the celebrated Hahnemann; this enlivened the public debate even further, especially when Hahnemann declined to visit him, so the Prince arranged to come to Leipzig. Whatever Hahnemann's reasons were he would have been unable to treat the Prince in Austria in any case because of the existing ban on the practise of homoeopathy.

The Prince improved considerably under Hahnemann's treatment and even wrote to his cousin, King Friedrich of Saxony, in an attempt to prevent the ban on Hahnemann becoming official. The improvement was temporary, however, because the Prince succumbed to his old drinking habits as well as the insistences of his personal physicians that venesections were necessary. Hahnemann refused to have anything more to do with the Prince when he discovered this. In October 1820 the Prince died and the post mortem confirmed the cause to be a stroke. The medical establishment lost no time in declaring that Hahnemann had hastened his death by neglecting to employ the necessary powerful measures earlier in the treatment. The way therefore became clear for the apothecaries, backed by most of the doctors of Leipzig, to obtain the official prohibition of Hahnemann dispensing his own medicines. They were successful and it became impossible for Hahnemann to continue practising homoeopathy in Leipzig as he insisted on making his own medicines.

The movement against homoeopathy started to gain momentum and all homoeopathic practitioners began to suffer varying degrees of ostracism, acrimonious public attacks and active persecution. Prison sentences, fines and damaging publicity ruined many of the careers of Hahnemann's pupils. The elated apothecaries went further, and even attempted to have Hahnemann forcibly removed from the city. Although this action did not succeed, Hahnemann had already decided to leave for Köthen where he would be able to practise his method in peace and under the protection of the Grand Duke Ferdinand, a former patient and, like Hahnemann, a Freemason.

A precedent had been established, and several years after Hahnemann's death, examples of prejudice against homoeopathy still abounded. For instance, when cholera struck London in 1854 the Board of Health appointed a committee of medical men to collect the statistics of the treatment of the disease in the city. They were then supposed to report to parliament on the results of the various methods pursued in all the different institutions. When the report appeared, the returns of the homoeopathic hospital were altogether ignored. Lord Ebury, who was a convert to homoeopathy, created a stir over the omission and a separate paper was then issued containing the astonishingly successful results. Their mortality rate was only 16.4 per cent whereas elsewhere it was in excess of 50 per cent. The strangest part of this story is the reason put forward by the Board of Health in defence of their action '. . . that by introducing the returns of homoeopathic practitioners . . . they would give an unjustifiable sanction to an empirical practice, alike opposed to the maintenance of truth and to the progress of science.'

Examples of prejudice today are still easy to find. The Faculty of Homoeopathy, based at the Royal London Homoeopathic Hospital, was empowered by an act of Parliament in 1950 to grant postgraduate medical diplomas. Grants are given to most N.H.S. doctors who wish to further their careers by taking additional diplomas or degrees. However, although doctors have applied, no grants have ever been given to those wishing to obtain a postgraduate qualification in homoeopathy.

Hahnemann's Destructive Attitude

Whilst on the subject of prejudice, Hahnemann's unnecessary contribution to the reluctance of the medical profession to examine or even tolerate homoeopathy must be acknowledged. It is appropriate to quote part of an article written by Prof. Puchelt in 1819.

> However contradictory it may appear at first sight to attempt to cure diseases by remedies which produce similar effects, it must be admitted that the paradox disappears when more careful consideration is given to the question of homoeopathy than has hitherto been usually given by the opponents of homoeopathy. I believe, indeed, that the system would not have met with so much opposition, that on the contrary, it would even have been accepted and employed by a great number of physicians, if Hahnemann had not declared open war upon the whole existing medical art, for everyone who has lived and worked in it, knows it is *not* so entirely built on sand as Hahnemann maintains . . . With the hostile attitude assumed by him towards other doctors, some self-effacement is required to attain the point of view from which he may be justly judged, and what is usefully extracted from his teaching; we are apt to be prejudiced against him by many offensive expressions, which indeed may have been deserved by some, but certainly not all the thoughtful physicians against whom they were directed.

Hahnemann almost certainly hindered the progress of his method by adopting such an uncompromising and dogmatic position.

A further illustration of Hahnemann's unfortunate attitude concerned the establishment and eventual collapse of the homoeopathic hospital in Leipzig. Prior to its opening in 1833 there had been a rapid growth in the number of practising homoeopaths in Leipzig, some of whom were not entirely in accord with all of Hahnemann's teachings. A periodical was started in which they aired their opinions. Hahnemann, who was now in exile, lost no time in sending back articles which rebuked the rebels. However, when word reached him that Dr Müller, a homoeopathic physician, had treated a young girl with blood leeches before she died, he was no longer able to exercise even a modicum of restraint. The result was a blistering, vituperative attack on the rebels entitled 'A Word to the Half-Homoeopaths of Leipzig'. This was published not in the periodical but in the public press.

In view of this shattering public denunciation, the hospital opening was conducted in a strained atmosphere. Dr Müller, its first Director, soon resigned as the hospital suffered considerably as a result of the vicious debate, public and professional, which Hahnemann's letter precipitated.

A new Director was elected but after a visit in 1834, Hahnemann suddenly declared that he would run the hospital himself although he was nearly eighty and lived many miles away in Köthen. It was a disastrous autocratic action which contributed to the deteriorating reputation and financial situation of the hospital. The next few years were characterized by discord and strife amongst the staff. In fact, one of the many chief physicians, appropriately named Dr Fickel, confessed that he had only infiltrated the hospital so that he could discredit the method of homoeopathy. After several more directors had resigned, a worsening financial position reduced it to out-patients only. It finally closed in 1842.

Many subsequent homoeopaths adopted this dogmatic attitude. In the words of Dr Richard Hughes, the well-known British Homoeopath at the turn of the century:

> To hear some among us talk, it would seem as if homoeopathy (at any rate in their hands) could cure everything, and no other way of proceeding could cure anything. To deliver us from these faults, we need freer air and the less dense aggregation we should obtain by being transferred from our little encampment, into the general array of the profession.

Medical Developments

The latter part of the nineteenth century witnessed various developments in the theory of disease but it was the discoveries of Pasteur and Lister which dramatically altered disease concepts. As a result, the science of bacteriology flourished and people believed the ultimate cause of disease had been found. Treatments were therefore increasingly aimed at the destruction of germs and *sulphonamides* and later *antibiotics* proved to be effective and powerful germicides. There seemed to be no place in this revolution for the Hahnemannian concept of treating the individual and not the disease. In addition the time-consuming procedures which were necessary to arrive at the appropriate individual homoeopathic remedy were in sharp contrast to the relatively easy situation where the same drug could be administered to everyone suffering from a similar disease.

The situation is much the same today although the idea of helping the body resist disease through the stimulation of its sophisticated immunological system, as opposed to a direct attack on the germs, has become increasingly acceptable.

As with the apothecaries, there is not much money to be made from the manufacture of homoeopathic medicines. For this reason, the impetus homoeopathy needs is unlikely to come from the pharmaceutical companies. It is therefore up to doctors to assess it in an unbiased and scientific manner. It would perhaps be salutary to conclude with the fact that, aside from Hahnemann's homoeopathic principle, all of his ideas on the treatment of disease, considered radical at the time, have since been accepted by the medical establishment. For instance his rejection of venesection and the use of leeches, his ideas on the treatment of the insane, his emphasis on hygiene and the need for a proper diet and plenty of physical exercise.

9. The History and Present Position of Homoeopathy in Great Britain

Frederick Hervey Foster Quin (1799-1878) is credited with the introduction of the method of homoeopathy to Great Britain. He graduated from Edinburgh University in 1820 and was shortly afterwards, in 1821, appointed physician to the exiled Napoleon. Napoleon died, however, before Quin was able to set sail for St Helena. His intention of opening a practice in London was thwarted by ill-health, and he went to Europe as the travelling physician to the Duchess of Devonshire (he was reputed to have been her illegitimate son) and ended up starting a practice in Naples where there was a large colony of English residents.

He was apparently cured of a serious illness with homoeopathic treatment. This prompted him to visit Hahnemann in 1826. Shortly after this visit he was appointed physician to Queen Victoria's uncle, Prince Leopold of Saxe-Coburg (later King of Belgium) and travelled round Europe with the Prince's household for several years.

In 1832 he returned to Britain and set up a practice at 19 King Street in London. The combination of his excellent social connections and his charisma was devastating and he soon became a well-known physician and raconteur. He proved to be a very suitable apostle of the new method and rapidly attracted interested colleagues. In 1844 he formed the British Homoeopathic Society which he presided over until his death in 1878.

Homoeopathic dispensaries sprang up wherever the converts

settled. By 1857 it was estimated that there were more than 200 homoeopathic practitioners in Great Britain and in addition to the many homoeopathic dispensaries the London Homoeopathic Hospital had been opened in 1850.

Frederick Hervey Foster Quin

Orthodox medical practices in Britain during this period were the very ones which Hahnemann had rebelled against: venesection, complex prescriptions of strong drugs, especially purgatives and emetics and so on. However, the reaction of the medical establishment in Britain to the new method contrasted favourably with the conduct of medical men elsewhere.

A Dr Ringer conveyed many homoeopathic' medicines and methods into orthodox therapeutics but they were extensively modified to meet the prejudices of the old school of medicine. His book proved to be so popular that ten editions were published.

Nevertheless, even this spirit of tolerance had its limits. Homoeopathic physicians were excluded from almost all medical societies and to a great extent from any kind of professional mixing. A conspiracy of silence, with respect to the subject of homoeopathy, operated in most periodicals. Thus, homoeopaths in Britain were not openly persecuted but neither were they welcomed with open arms.

Homoeopathy has been linked with many famous people since its inception. Hahnemann himself treated members of the European royalty as well as Germany's beloved Goethe. Dr Quin in England is reputed to have had Dickens, Landseer and Thackeray amongst his many patients. Even today many famous names openly favour and support the practice of homoeopathy. For instance Yehudi Menuhin and Sir Adrian Boult are currently patrons of the British Homoeopathic Association.

Royal Connections

There is a very interesting connection between homoeopathy and the British monarchy. Queen Mary, consort of King George V is often credited with the introduction of homoeopathy to the Royal Family. However, the researches of Dr T. M. Cook have revealed a much earlier royal interest in the method. Queen Adelaide, consort of William IV, was known to have been a keen supporter of homoeopathy for most of her life. In fact she summoned Dr Stapf to Windsor Castle in 1835 to treat her. Dr Stapf, a close friend of Hahnemann's, was, at that time, the Medical Councillor for Saxony. He had become a celebrated homoeopathic physician and, prior to this summons, had been treating Queen Adelaide by post.

When Prince Albert married Queen Victoria in 1840 the Royal patronage of homoeopathy was continued as there was a strong homoeopathic tradition in his family. Queen Adelaide was in fact Prince Albert's aunt, and further homoeopathic influence may well have come via Queen Victoria's uncle, Prince Leopold. It will be recalled that Dr Quin had been personal physician to the Prince and his household prior to setting up a practice in London.

From the time that Dr John Weir, a homoeopathic practitioner, was appointed as physician to King George V and Queen Mary, to the present day, the allegiance of the Royal Family to homoeopathy has, if anything, become stronger. Edward VIII was said to have invariably carried certain homoeopathic remedies on his person. King George VI was a very keen advocate of the method having been cured by Dr Weir of the seasickness which had plagued him since childhood. His family, the Royal household, and even his cattle all became the beneficiaries of his increasing knowledge and enthusiasm as he often prescribed homoeopathic remedies for them. One of his racehorses was named 'Hypericum', after an important homoeopathic remedy, and the horse went on to grace the name of homoeopathy by winning the 1,000 Guinea Stakes at Newmarket in 1946. Although the King died at the early age of 57, he is said to have told friends that he firmly believed homoeopathy had extended his life. H.M. Queen Elizabeth the Queen Mother, H.M. Queen Elizabeth II and her family all continue to echo King George VI's support for homoeopathy.

The Growing Kentian Influence
Until 1902, when Dr Richard Hughes died, homoeopathy in Britain had for some time been completely dominated by his powerful character and intellect. He and his fellow stalwarts believed they had correctly interpreted Hahnemannian homoeopathy although he admitted the following:

> We are homoeopathists not Hahnemannians. Homoeopathy is a vital thing. It is in our hands somewhat different from what it was when it dropped from Hahnemann's; but it is Hahnemann's still. All study, exposition, practice of it must start from him; and the result it achieves must be accounted a monument reared to his honour.

Hughes accepted the Hahnemannian aim of matching the totality of the patient's symptoms as far as possible with the drug picture. However, he considered the pathological symptoms and their modalities to be of prime importance; the mental and general symptoms serving mainly as a confirmation or confutation of an indicated remedy. He also used only the lower potencies and remained thoroughly sceptical of potencies greater than 30c. Although Hughes was unable to explain how potentization enhanced the curative effects of a drug he was prepared to accept the phenomenon on the basis of clinical evidence. However, as he lived in an era dominated by the concept of the absolute and indivisible atom, his scientific integrity prevented him from embracing the potencies above which atoms of the remedy ceased to be present. He did, however, acknowledge to a certain extent, the clinical evidence supporting the activity of some of the higher potencies up to 200c. When it became apparent that the American School of Homoeopaths, led by Drs Kent and Allen, were using potencies of 1M (1000c), 10M (10,000c) and CM (100,000c) he was sufficiently outraged to refer to these potencies as 'airy nothings'.

The followers of Hughes were soon unable to curtail the growing Kentian influence amongst the British homoeopathic doctors. Kent's book entitled *Lectures on the Materia Medica*, published in 1904, was written in colloquial style at the request of his students. It was thus very readable; an adjective one could not use to describe previous *Materia Medica* publications, and indeed Hughes' monumental and scholarly work on the *Materia Medica*. The drug pictures in Kent's book contained descriptions of the particular type of person which each remedy suited. The vogue of prescribing principally on a person's constitutional symptoms began with these drug descriptions.

Dr Margaret Tyler, a devoted disciple of Kent, was the first British doctor to infiltrate the ranks of the old school. Concerned at the lack of homoeopathic training facilities, she set up, with her mother's help, a trust which enabled British doctors to go to Chicago and study there under Kent. Dr John Weir, who was converted to homoeopathy when he was cured of a septic infection by H.M. Gibson Millar, the famous Glasgow homoeopath, was awarded the first Henry Tyler Scholarship.

He came back from Chicago enthusiastic and convinced of the value of constitutional prescribing and the use of high potencies.

Weir's influence gradually increased, and more and more doctors practised the form of homoeopathy advocated by Kent. By 1924, only one of the 'old Guard' remained and British homoeopathy had more or less completed its transition to the Kentian interpretation of homoeopathy, an interpretation which still reigns supreme today. Weir's appointment as physician to King George V was followed in 1932 by a Knighthood. In 1937 he was appointed as a physician to King George VI. On his retirement as Royal Homoeopathic Physician he was succeeded by Dr Margery Blackie, the first woman doctor to be appointed by a reigning monarch. She, in turn, has been succeeded by Dr C. K. Elliot.

The Faculty of Homoeopathy and The Royal London Homoeopathic Hospital

The institutions associated with homoeopathy have suffered various fates. The British Homoeopathy Society founded by Dr Quin became the Faculty of Homoeopathy in 1943. It was empowered in 1950, by an Act of Parliament, to award postgraduate diplomas in homoeopathy. However, despite consistent pressure, the British Medical Council have remained firm in their resolve not to recognize this diploma. Courses, which are generally run by the Faculty for medical doctors only, are preparatory for the diploma examination. Success in this examination entitles the doctor to a membership of the Faculty of Homoeopathy (M.F.Hom.) Veterinary and dental surgeons, Pharmacists and State Registered Nurses may become associates but not members of the Faculty.

The Royal London Homoeopathic Hospital, which is closely associated with the Faculty, has survived the threat of closure several times. It was founded by Dr F. H. Quin in 1849, and soon built up a considerable reputation. It moved to its present site in Great Ormond Street in 1859. The hospital was badly damaged during the second world war but was rebuilt and encorporated into the National Health Service when it was inaugurated in 1948. In the same year it became the 'Royal London Homoeopathic Hospital' by command of H.M. King George VI. It celebrated its centenary the following year and King George

VI joined in the celebrations and expressed 'the earnest hope that it may long maintain its record of achievement.' Aneurin Bevan, and successive Ministers of Health, have all given assurances that homoeopathic medicine will always be available on the N.H.S.

Initially it was governed by its own Management Committee, but under the 1973 Reorganization Act it became part of the Camden and Islington Area Health Authority. In 1979 plans were afoot to severely limit the work of the hospital. However, a petition containing 116,848 signatures and a mass lobby of Parliament staved off the impending threat. This only proved to be temporary for its operating theatre has recently been condemned along with its future as a general hospital. Fortunately Tom Ellis M.P. has espoused the cause of homoeopathy and is determined to maintain the hospital as a general teaching hospital, and to ensure that the promise to keep homoeopathy available on the N.H.S. is fulfilled. The Homoeopathic Trust has agreed to contribute a substantial sum of money towards the modernization of the theatres and it seems that the hospital has survived, once more, a threat to its very existence.

Other hospitals providing in-patient and out-patient facilities within the N.H.S. are: The Bristol Homoeopathic Hospital, the Tunbridge Wells Homoeopathic Hospital and the Glasgow Homoeopathic Hospital, which also runs post-graduate courses. The Glasgow Homoeopathic Hospital for Children was unfortunately closed at the end of November 1979. With the reorganization of the N.H.S. on Merseyside the Liverpool Hahnemann Hospital was closed in 1976. Facilities are now available in that city at the Mossley Hill Hospital for out-patients only. There are various other homoeopathic clinics throughout Britain which only cater for out-patients.

The limited availability of homoeopathic treatment on the N.H.S., in conjunction with a rapidly growing public demand for homoeopathy, has led to an increase in the number of private homoeopathic doctors. The latest figures show that there are approximately 180 private homoeopathic doctors, 15 N.H.S. doctors who practise homoeopathy full time, and about 140 N.H.S. doctors who practise homoeopathy to a limited extent only. One of the drawbacks of private practice is that

The Royal London Homoeopathic Hospital

relatively few of the homoeopathic doctors are recognized by the private health insurance companies.

Homoeopathic Pharmacies
Two companies in England are under licence to manufacture homoeopathic remedies: A. Nelson & Co. and Weleda U.K. Ltd. Chemists throughout the country are responding to the resurgence of public interest and the demand for homoeopathic treatment by stocking a range of homoeopathic remedies. In fact between 1980 and 1981 the number of chemists stocking homoeopathic remedies doubled from approximately 150 to 300.

Homoeopathic Societies
The Homoeopathic Trust, the Homoeopathic Development Foundation, the Hahnemann Society, the British Homoeopathic Association as well as the many local homoeopathic groups which are being formed throughout the country, all seek to promulgate the method of homoeopathy. Any enquiries concerning homoeopathy and its availability in Great Britain should be directed to one or other of these organizations (see Useful Addresses on page 126).

10. What Can Homoeopathy Be Used to Treat?

There is no condition which homoeopathy cannot be used to treat. While it may not be able to cure cases of advanced chronic illness it can often alleviate the suffering and thus improve the quality of the patient's life. Additionally it can be safely used as an adjunct to orthodox treatment without fear of harmful interactions or toxic side-effects. This is to the patient's advantage for it means that he can undergo homoeopathic treatment without having to stop all orthodox drugs immediately. Many people find that they are able to reduce or even stop their intake of conventional drugs as a result of having homoeopathic treatment. It is, however, unfortunate that most people view the homoeopathic method as the last possible resort for difficult, chronic diseases which have not responded to any other form of treatment. The good results achieved through homoeopathy seem even more remarkable when one considers that the bulk of a homoeopath's patients consist of these resistant cases, given up as hopeless by the medical profession.

While homoeopathic remedies can be taken with orthodox drugs, the latter may inhibit their action to a certain extent. This is to be expected as homoeopathic remedies are presumed to work by stimulating the body's natural defences whereas most allopathic drugs work through the suppression of these defences. For this reason, children and adults who have not been taking conventional drugs for any length of time usually respond exceptionally well to homoeopathic treatment.

Although homoeopathy can be employed in any condition, it is important to bear in mind Hahnemann's instruction to seek out and exclude, if possible, any exciting or contributing factors to the fundamental causes of disease. It is worthwhile quoting Hahnemann on this matter as people often forget his wise words and see homoeopathy in isolation from all other therapeutic approaches:

> The age of the patient, his mode of living and diet, his occupation, his domestic position, his social relations and so forth, must next be taken into consideration in order to ascertain whether these things have tended to increase his malady, or in how far they may favour or hinder the treatment. Likewise, the state of his disposition and mind must be attended to, to learn whether that presents any obstacle to the treatment, or requires to be directed, encouraged or modified.

Homoeopathy can be employed to great effect in the treatment of acute infections. Although antibiotics represent powerful and effective weapons against these disorders they are not without their disadvantages. Micro-organisms are notorious for their phenomenal ability to acquire resistance to antibiotics. New varieties are constantly being developed in order to combat this problem which is becoming increasingly apparent because of their large-scale, often indiscriminate, usage. The more they are used the sooner the organisms will acquire immunity. In addition, they are not without their side-effects. Some people are so sensitive to certain types that they can die because of a severe allergic reaction to them. They cause disturbances in the bowel flora, increase the likelihood of fungal infections and are associated with numerous other complications. Most homoeopathic remedies prove to be remarkably successful in clearing up sore throats, fevers, colds, chest infections, tonsillitis, ear infections and so forth.

It must be stressed that certain orthodox drugs should only be discontinued under medical supervision even if homoeopathic treatment is being used concurrently.

Many cases of asthma, hay fever and catarrhal diseases have been cured with homoeopathy. Careful attention should also be given to the type of foods eaten by the patient as this can be an important contributing factor in these and many other diseases.

Gastro-intestinal disorders such as diarrhoea, constipation, colitis, piles, acute vomiting, dyspepsia, and peptic ulcer are all conditions which can respond very well to homoeopathic treatment; frequently resulting in a permanent cure.

Headaches are very amenable to homoeopathic treatment and it is not unusual for cures to be obtained even in patients who have had intractable migraine for many years.

Rheumatic diseases are one of the main causes of disability and loss of working hours today. If these are treated early there is a good chance that a permanent cure can be achieved with homoeopathic treatment. This is, however, unlikely in the advanced stages of these chronic diseases as irreversible physical processes have usually occurred. Nevertheless, homoeopathic remedies can frequently effect similar, if not greater, improvement when compared with conventional treatment. This is important in view of the fact that some patients cannot tolerate certain orthodox drugs because of severe reactions to them.

Skin diseases such as eczema, dermatitis, psoriasis can be helped with homoeopathy although a long course of treatment is often required. Additionally boils, abscesses, acne, rosacea and shingles respond favourably to homoeopathy. The improvement gained in this manner is usually permanent and is not therefore limited to the duration of the treatment as is often the case for many conventional treatments such as steroid creams.

Menstrual problems including dysmenorrhoea, ammenorrhoea as well as symptoms associated with the menopause respond well to homoeopathy. Both chronic and acute cystitis, nephritis and vaginal discharges can clear up completely with homoeopathic treatment.

As already stated, Hahnemann believed that various mental as well as physical symptoms could be indicative of underlying disease processes. Thus, some mental conditions can be greatly alleviated or even cured with appropriate homoeopathic treatment. Due attention must be given to obvious causal factors which should be excluded if possible. However, patients suffering from varying degrees of anxiety and depression have often been dramatically helped by homoeopathic treatment even though precipitating causes have not been removed. This is because homoeopathic treatment can improve the patient's feeling of well-being to such an extent that his ability to cope with stressful situations is also improved.

Indeed, it is true to say that there is no medical condition for which homoeopathy cannot offer some help. There is still, obviously, a need for replacement therapy in deficiency diseases, psychotherapy, dietetic, manipulation (osteopathy and chiropractic), physiotherapy and surgery. However, none of these treatments need exclude homoeopathy. For instance, many homoeopathic physicians believe that appropriate remedies can definitely improve a patient's rate of recovery from an operation. On many occasions, however, patients have been taken off the operating list when awaiting surgery following successful homoeopathic treatment. Generally, these have only been cases for minor surgery such as piles, varicose veins etc., but some people with peptic ulcers or even ulcerative colitis have escaped the need for major surgery.

It is impossible to give statistics regarding the effectiveness of homoeopathy in different conditions. This is due to the problems peculiar to homoeopathy, which are discussed elsewhere. However, it is fair to say that most homoeopathic doctors have seen homoeopathy effect dramatic cures and improvements sufficiently often to lay the onus of failure on their particular choice of remedy rather than the method itself. This is why a homoeopathic doctor will rarely, if ever, be heard to say 'there is nothing more I can do for you.'

11. Examples of Some Commonly Used Remedies

This chapter is the result of an optimistic notion that the preceding chapters will have left the reader with a strong desire to experiment with the homoeopathic method. Although more serious conditions should be seen and treated by a homoeopathic physician there are a multitude of less serious, yet bothersome, ailments which can be effectively treated at home. It is interesting to note that homoeopathic general practitioners have all found that patients who do a lot of their own prescribing require far fewer surgery and home visits, especially with regard to their children.

Before various remedies are described in detail it is worth listing the advantages of the homoeopathic method aside from its proven record of effectiveness.

(1) *Toxicity*. Homoeopathic remedies are considered to be non-toxic and therefore harmless. This statement must, however, be qualified for two reasons:

(a) The low potencies still contain the remedies in a material dose and if taken over a fairly long period of time could produce some of the effects associated with that drug.

(b) Homoeopathic 'aggravations', discussed elsewhere, do occur in a very small minority and thus one cannot say emphatically that homoeopathic remedies are without side-effects.

(2) *Rapidity of Action*. In acute situations, the relief obtained from the appropriate homoeopathic remedy is often instant-

aneous. *Aconite* and *Belladonna* can reduce fevers in a matter of minutes. Likewise migraine and hay fever can respond to the correct remedy within seconds.

(3) *Administration*. Most homoeopathic remedies are taken orally but since a few granules placed on the tongue or on the inside of the mouth are rapidly absorbed it is not essential for them to be swallowed. This means that cases of coma, epilepsy and repeated vomiting for example can still be treated homoeopathically.

(4) *Acceptability*. Since the base of all remedies is either lactose or sucrose they are eagerly swallowed by children, adults and even animals.

(5) *Shelf life*. Homoeopathic remedies remain active indefinitely. However, they should not be contaminated through over-handling, nor exposed to sunlight or strong volatile oils. Neither should they be moved from one container to another. It is wise to observe these precautions as it is believed that all of these actions can destroy the 'activity' of the remedies.

(6) *Economy*. Homoeopathic remedies are cheap and can be obtained through the N.H.S. Prescribing costs of full-time N.H.S. homoeopathic practitioners are consistently well below the national average.

(7) *Simplicity*. Finally, but perhaps most importantly, homoeopathy is not enshrouded in mystery. It outlines a basic and simple method which enables one to choose a specific remedy in a specific situation. Lay people who are interested and concerned about their health can therefore quickly learn how to treat their own, less serious complaints. Many families who treat themselves will readily admit the gratification that accompanies treating and relieving various complaints without recourse to strong conventional drugs.

The following remedies will be listed alphabetically and whenever modalities are included the abbreviations found in a homoeopathic *Materia Medica* will be used. For example if a symptom is worse for heat and better for pressure it will be written as follows: < heat, > pressure. The symbols are self-explanatory.

Aconite

This remedy is always called for when trembling, breathlessness, palpitations, pain, fear, panic and distress accompany the folllowing situations:

Any mental or physical shock, for instance, bereavement, a traffic accident, falling down the stairs, being bitten by an animal etc.

Asthma. Dry suffocating cough.

Colds and sore throats following exposure to cold dry winds.

Haemorrhage.

At the onset of a fever if the temperatures are high and the patient is restless and very thirsty.

Teething; gums hot and inflamed.

Symptoms < lying on affected side
                 warm room
                 tobacco smoke
                 cold winds
                 at night
           > open air
                 when the bed clothes are thrown off

Aconite is only suitable in acute conditions for although its effect is powerful, the duration is only short.

Arnica

For any injuries—bruises, sprains, concussion.

Physical exhaustion following a hard day's work, such as gardening, a long hike etc. Swiss mountain guides still chew Arnica leaves to prevent and remove muscle aching and soreness.

After surgery and childbirth—can also be taken before as a prophylactic to prevent bruising.

Bed feels too hard, constant desire to move to a softer spot.

Symptoms < least touch
                 motion
                 cold, damp situations
           > lying down
                 head low

Aconite and Arnica are indicated in roughly 80 per cent of all accidents and emergencies and initial experiments with these two remedies should guarantee your conversion to homoeopathy.

Arsenicum Album (Arsen. alb.)

This remedy is especially indicated when the patient is very chilly, fearful, restless and exhausted.

Acute gastro-enteritis, especially if vomiting occurs during the diarrhoea. Exhaustion after diarrhoea.

Food poisoning.

Cannot bear the sight or smell of food.

Great thirst but patient only wants to sip little and often.

Breathing difficult with need to sit or bend forward.

Burning pains in all parts. Throat, stomach etc.

Symptoms   <   after midnight, mid-morning and between 1-2 p.m.
cold wet weather.
      >   heat but with cool air around the head.

Belladonna

This remedy is indicated when the symptoms come on suddenly and violently. There is always great heat, burning, redness and throbbing. The face is often very flushed, the pupils dilated, the pulse pounding and the patient can be very excited, if not delirious.

Severe throbbing earache, headache, boils or sore throat, especially when accompanied by the above symptoms.

Neuralgic pains which come and go suddenly.

Dry throat and mouth but refuses to drink.

Effects of sun exposure.

Symptoms   <   afternoon
night
noise
touch
lying down
      >   warmth
sitting erect

This is an excellent children's remedy and one of the main ones employed in fevers.

Bryonia

The key characteristics of this remedy are an aggravation of all symptoms following movement and dryness of mucous and serous membranes.

Bursting headaches, migraine.

Arthritis.

Dryness. Dry painful cough, often violent. Dry mouth. Dry lips. Dry crumbling stool.

Thirsty especially for cold drinks.

Irritable.

Pain and discomfort in the stomach, too painful to touch.

Symptoms < any movement
                 warmth
           > from cold
                 pressure (except abdomen)
                 rest
                 lying on painful side

Camphor

This remedy is valuable when the whole body is icy cold especially following a chill.

First stage of a cold where there is sneezing and a feeling of coldness.

Patient will not be covered despite coldness of the body.

Diarrhoea with coldness of the body.

Symptoms < motion
                 night
                 contact
                 cold air
           > warmth

Cantharis

This is an important cystitis remedy and can bring immediate relief of symptoms. However, the patient should always attend a clinic so that a full investigation can be conducted.

Raw, burning pains generally. Can be in the bladder, mouth, throat, chest or rectum.

Intolerable urge to urinate all the time. The urine scalds and only passes drop by drop.

Any burns and scalds before blisters have formed.

Cantharis can be applied locally in tincture form, taken internally in potency or both.

Sun burn.

Gnat bites.

Excessive sexual desire.

Symptoms   <   touch
                  urinating
                  cold water
                  coffee

Carbo vegetabilis (Carbo veg.)

For use in situations where feelings of sluggishness, puffiness, distention and fullness predominate.

Indigestion with excessive flatulence. Temporary relief is gained from bringing up wind.

Collapse or fainting with cold face, cold sweat and breath.

Other ill-effects of exhausting illnesses. *Carbo veg.* is also known as the 'corpse reviver'.

Burnings internally in veins, head, stomach but with icy coldness of face, breath, knees and feet.

Hoarseness, whooping cough, asthma.

Symptoms   <   after eating fatty foods
                  warm damp weather
                  evening and night
              >   after bringing up wind
                  from fanning

Chamomilla

Especially suited to childhood complaints when the child is sensitive, irritable, impatient, thirsty, hot and numb. Mental calmness always contra-indicates *Chamomilla*.

All pains are unbearable. Earache, toothache, teething.

Colic, especially with green motions.

Irritable dry tickling cough.

One cheek is often red and hot, the other cool.

Symptoms   <   heat
                  anger
                  open air
                  night
              >   being carried about
                  warm wet weather

Cuprum

This can be an excellent remedy for cramps, spasms and convulsions.

Whooping cough with blue face. Violent spasmodic cough with shortness of breath.

Nausea with stomach pain.

Strong metallic taste in the mouth. Craves cool drinks.

Symptoms < vomiting
during menses
contact
evening and night
cold air
> while perspiring
cold water

Drosera

This remedy is chiefly employed in the treatment of coughs.

Whooping cough or any cough with sudden violent attacks which often end in vomiting.

Constant tickling cough. Sensation of a feather in the throat.

Laryngitis with a dry throat which makes talking an effort.

Symptoms < after midnight
from lying down
from the warmth of the bed
drinking
laughing
singing

Euphrasia

This remedy should be given at the onset of measles if the eyes are streaming, the tears burn and the person cannot tolerate bright light.

For colds and hay fever with watering eyes and streaming nose.

Inflamed eyes which water, sting and burn.

Conjunctivitis, intolerance of bright light.

Sneezing cough.

Throbbing headache.

Symptoms <   indoors
                warmth
                evenings
                bright light
           >   dim light/darkness
                cold applications

Gelsemium

This remedy is frequently employed in the treatment of colds and nervousness.

Nervousness and worry, especially if precedes all tasks, minor or major.

Influenza; patient is hot-flushed, trembling, dizzy and drowsy. Weary with aching muscles, sneezing and running nose. Tight headache, feeling of a band around the head.

Sore throat, difficulty swallowing. Absence of thirst even with a very high temperature.

During fever wants to be held to prevent the marked trembling.

In measles if most of the above symptoms correspond.

Symptoms <   damp weather
                emotion
                excitement
                thinking of ailments
           >   open air
                after urinating
                continued motion
                stimulants

Ipecacuahna

This remedy is indicated in any illness which is characterized by constant nausea, vomiting, a clean tongue and copious amounts of saliva. These can be:

Asthma where the chest is full of phlegm which is difficult to expectorate.

Incessant violent coughing with every breath, plus wheezing. Bronchitis.

Nose bleeds, haemorrhages.

Symptoms <   lying down
                periodically

Nux vomica

Nux vomica is often suitable if patients are irritable, impatient and quarrelsome. Oversensitive to noise, odours, light and music. Trifling ailments become unbearable.

Great feeling of chilliness. In fever the body can be burning hot, especially face, yet the patient cannot move or be uncovered without feeling chilly.

Ill-effects of over indulgence in food and alcohol. Can often remove a hang-over.

There is pain and distention in the stomach two to three hours after eating.

Constipation with ineffectual urging or the feeling as if part of the stool remains unexpelled. Absence of all desire to defecate is a contra-indication for *Nux vomica*.

Itching piles.

Nausea with much retching, difficult to empty stomach.

Stuffy colds which are worse in cold air. Infant's snuffles if he is extremely irritable.

Raw throat.

Early morning violent cough which can precipitate a bursting headache.

Dysmenorrhoea with pain in sacrum and constant urging to stool.

Fussy over food. Likes rich fatty foods. Dislikes coffee and tobacco smoke.

Symptoms < cold
between 3-4 a.m.
morning
mental exertion
after spices and stimulants
> evening
being covered
warmth
after a short sleep if unaroused

Pulsatilla

This remedy is characterized by symptoms which are constantly changing. For instance, rheumatic pains which shift rapidly from one place to another. Happy one moment, miserable the next etc.

Weepiness.

Seeks the open air, always feels better there. Unhappy in warm stuffy atmospheres.

Yellow-green thick catarrh of eyelids or nose.

Eyes sore, red, itchy, styes. Crack in middle of lower lip.

Catarrhal cough. Loss of taste and smell.

Otitis media where there is a thick bland discharge.

Measles, especially with coughing, sore eyes, catarrh and tendency to ear and chest complications.

Mumps.

Menses suppressed or delayed. When they are scanty yet protracted.

Aversion to fatty greasy food which upsets the stomach.

Absence of thirst during fever even though the mouth may be very dry.

Menopause.

Symptoms < heat, stuffy atmospheres
                 rich fatty foods
                 sudden chilling
            > cold applications, especially rheumatic
                 pains
                 open air
                 cold food and drink
                 lying on painful side

Opium

This remedy is included in the list because one of the main and well-proven side-effects of opiate and opiate derivative drugs is constipation. It is frequently indicated in constipation characterized by complete inactivity, that is, where there is no pain, no urging and no discomfort.

Inactivity of bladder. Retention with full bladder.

Painless symptoms, e.g. ulcers which are not painful.

Drowsy stupor, general sluggishness.

Sleepy but sleeplessness. Hypersensitive to all noises, can hear 'flies walking on the wall' etc.

Ailments from fright—where fear remains a long time after.

Bed feels too hot—wants to move to a cool place or to be uncovered.

Rhus toxicodendron
This is a very useful rheumatic remedy and is also of value in certain skin eruptions. The characteristic modality of this remedy is particularly striking. The symptoms are worse on first moving but relieved by sustained and gentle movement.

In the treatment of any part of the body which is painful or stiff and is characterized by this modality.

Restlessness, must move the aching part.

Dryness of mouth with great thirst; red triangular tip of tongue.

Effects of over-exertion. Over-use of voice which is initially hoarse but then improves with continued use.

Skin eruptions which are vesicular or pustular.

Shingles, chicken-pox and herpes.

Eczema, especially of palms and fingers.

Symptoms <   on beginning to move
                    from cold to wet
                    during rest
                    at night and after midnight
          >   with continued, gentle movement
                    from warm applications
                    during warm weather

Sulphur
This remedy is particularly valuable in certain skin complaints.

Skin is dry and unhealthy-looking. Every injury tends to suppurate. All skin complaints are characteristically burning and itchy.

Boils, abscesses, severe acne, eczema, dermatitis, psoriasis.

Feet burn in bed, must put them outside blankets to cool off.

Hot flushes especially at menopause.

Red, burning orifices: lips, anus, nose, vulva.

Offensive body odour, person often offended by his own smell.

Chronic dry catarrh, irritating discharge from nose.

Diarrhoea which often drives people from bed in the morning.

Burning stool.

Likes sweets, fatty foods and stimulants.

Milk disagrees.

Empty sinking sensation around 11 a.m., relieved by snacking.

Easily fatigued.

Dislike of washing and bathing which usually aggravates their symptoms.

Symptoms < standing
         after sleep
         after eating
         night
         warmth of bed, and heat in general
         bathing
         11 a.m.
    > dry warm weather
         lying on right side

Since the most commonly available potency in Great Britain is 6c, it is probably advisable to experiment with this potency first. In acute conditions take the remedy every few hours or more frequently with particularly distressing symptoms. It is useful to eventually have most remedies available in different potencies so that others can be tried when a certain one fails to have any effect.

Many of the symptoms described in these brief remedy descriptions could be regarded as fairly serious. One must be sensible, but in many cases it is possible to treat and relieve the patient's symptoms before the doctor is even able to see him.

It only remains to conclude with the sincere hope that your initial experiments with the homoeopathic method will be successful and gratifying and will encourage a deeper exploration into this gentle therapeutic method.

Bibliography

Ameke, W. *History of Homoeopathy*, E. Gould and Son, 1885.

Boyd, Hamish. *Introduction to Homoeopathic Medicine*, Beaconsfield Publishers Ltd., 1981.

Cook, Trevor M. *Samuel Hahnemann: The Founder of Homoeopathic Medicine*, Thorsons Publishers Ltd., 1981.

Hahnemann, Samuel. *Organon of Medicine*, Boericke & Tafel, Philadelphia, 1952.

Hughes, R. *Principles and Practice of Homoeopathy*, Leath and Ross, 1902.

Jack, R. A. F. *Introducing Homoeopathy into General Practice*, A. Small.

Wheeler, C. *Introduction to the Principles and Practice of Homoeopathy*, Health Service Press, 1948.

Nelsons. *The Homoeopathic Handbook 1981.*

Article references from the British Homoeopathic Journal:
Bodman, F. 'Winds of Change from Chicago' (January 1980).

Campbell, A. 'Should We Resurrect R. Hughes?' (April 1980).

——. 'Thuja—a Drug Picture Based on Provings' (October 1980).

——. 'The Background of Provings and Current Implications' (January 1981).

——. 'The Concept of Constitution in Homoeopathy' (October 1981).

Foubister, D. M. 'Constitutional Types' (October 1981).

Gibson, R. G. et al. 'The Place for Non-pharmaceutical Therapy in Chronic Rheumatoid Arthritis: a Critical Study of Homoeopathy' (July 1980).

Jones, L. and Jenkins, M. D. 'Plant Responses to Homoeopathic Remedies' (July 1981).

Kennedy, C. O. 'Richard Hughes in 1972' (January 1973).

McKinlay Burns, I. 'The Value of the Low Potencies' (April 1972).

Mitchel, G. R. 'Hughes, Hahnemann and the Half Homoeopaths' (July 1976).

Rawson, D. S. 'A Scientific Approach to Homoeopathy' (April 1972).

Savage, R. H. 'The Unrecognized Use of Homoeopathy in Conventional Medicine' (April 1980).

Stephenson, J. 'Substances in Dilutions Greater Than 10' (January 1973).

Ustianowski, P. A. 'A Clinical Trial of Staphysagria in Post Coital Cystitis' (October 1974).

Von Keller, G. 'Lilium and the Relative Value of Symptoms' (January 1981).

——. 'Chelidonium and Organ Therapy' (July 1981).

Useful Reference Books

Allen, H. C. *Keynotes and Characteristics of Leading Remedies*, Thorsons Publishers Ltd.

Blackie, Margery. *The Patient Not the Cure*, Macdonald (1975).

Borland, D. M. *Homoeopathy in Practice*, Beaconsfield Publishers Ltd.

Boericke, W. *Materia Medica with Repertory*, Boericke and Runyon (Philadelphia).

Clarke, J. H. *Clinical Repertory*, C. W. Daniel Co. Ltd.

Hahnemann, S. *Materia Medica Pura.*

Hering, C. *Condensed Materia Medica*, Boericke and Tafel (New York).

Hughes, R. *A Manual of Pharmacodynamics.*

——. *Principles and Practice of Homoeopathy*, Leath and Ross, 1902.

Kent, J. T. *Repertory of Homoeopathic Materia Medica.*

Pratt, N. J. *Homoeopathic Prescribing*, Beaconsfield Publishers Ltd.

Tyler, M. L. *Homoeopathic Drug Pictures*, C. W. Daniel Co. Ltd.

Useful Addresses

The Faculty of Homoeopathy
The Royal London Homoeopathic Hospital
Great Ormond Street
London WC1N 3HR
(Tel. 01-837 3091)

The Homoeopathic Development Foundation
Harcourt House
19a Cavendish Square
London W1M 9AD
(Tel. 01-629 3205)

The British Homoeopathic Association
Basildon Court
27a Devonshire Street
London W1N 1RJ
(Tel. 01-935 2163)

The Hahnemann Society
Human Education Centre
Avenue Lodge
Bounds Green Road
London N22 4EU
(Tel. 01-889 1595)

Index